Being Medicine

A SHAMANIC GUIDE TO MYSTICAL
WEALTH + MANIFESTATION

JULIET TRNKA

Being Medicine:
A Shamanic Guide to Mystical Wealth + Manifestation

Copyright © 2023 by Juliet Trnka

All rights reserved. No part of this publication may be reproduced, distributed, or transmitted in any form or by any means, including photocopying, recording or other electronic or mechanical methods, without the prior written permission of the author, except in the case of brief quotations embodied in reviews and certain other non-commercial uses permitted by copyright law.

Printed in the United States of America
Hardcover ISBN: 978-1-960876-30-0
Paperback ISBN: 978-1-960876-31-7
Ebook ISBN: 978-1-960876-32-4
Library of Congress Control Number: 2023944876

Muse Literary
3319 N. Cicero Avenue
Chicago IL 60641-9998

*I remember you, remembering me, remembering you.
I remember that you are a revolution, expressing in skin,
blood and bone.
May this book remember you home to what is wild and
unconditioned in you.
May it feralize you out of conformity.
May it illuminate that which is dangerous and deserving in you.
Let this book deliver us to where we remember well and
are remembered well.*

Table of Contents

Introduction. vii

Chapter 1: Desire: Offer You for the Destiny of All. 1
   Poems of Desire 7
   Desire Ritual 37
   Journal Prompts for Desire. 38

Chapter 2: Decision: Let Your Destiny Live 39
   Poems of Decision 46
   Ritual to Bless Decision 67
   Journal Prompts for Decision. 68

Chapter 3: Surrender: Unguard Your Destiny 69
   Poems of Surrender 78
   Ritual of Surrender. 100
   Journal Prompts for Surrender 101

Chapter 4: Inspired Action: Demonstrate Your Destiny . . .103
   Poems of Inspired Action 111
   Ritual of Inspired Action 128
   Journal Prompts for Inspired Action. 129

Chapter 5: Receiving: Have Your Destiny Now..........131
    Poems of Receiving............................143
    Ritual for Receiving 171
    Journal Prompts for Receiving 172

Epilogue...173
    Ritual for Closure.............................175

About the Author..................................177

Introduction

It was 5:30 in the morning, the sun barely peeking out over the mountains. Held in the sweet liminal realm between sleep and awake, I had a vision that I'll never forget. It was the full illumination of my purpose.

I went to bed the night before as many high-achieving women do, bringing the whole world to bed with me. I was in the middle of a massive growth spurt in my business, and the intensity of meeting a higher revenue goal than ever before had me hot and restless. Though I know from experience that the question, *How can this possibly work?* is not one that can support the kind of leap I was initiating, it kept pinging through my brain each time I was about to drift off.

But then something unexplainable happened. Inwardly I turned toward that goal and all it implied. I dropped the *how* and connected to the deep well of meaning this goal had for me. The greater freedom, the larger space for mystical experiences, all the surprising gifts I knew come from these leaps that I couldn't yet imagine. The sweet relief of knowing my projects are funded. The play and laughter that would flow even more easily.

I dropped the *how* and simply said *yes*.

Inside of this yes, I finally fell asleep.

In the dreamy half-dark hours of the next morning, the vision came.

I was first shown a moment from my childhood. I am four years old, in our backyard under a crabapple tree in the early morning. I see a small robin on the ground in front of me and move quietly and carefully towards it. I get closer and closer, my little heart fluttering. I reach down to pick the bird up. I am able to scoop it up into my tiny hands and hold it at my chest, feeling its heart racing as fast as my own. I feel an intense joy, and at the same time, a deep fear that I'll get in trouble or that I might hurt the bird somehow. I release it, and it flies away.

The vision carried me to a second moment. I am eighteen years old and sitting on the mountain peak of Huayna Picchu in Peru. I feel the rising heat of the early morning sun as it climbs up my back. No one else is here or in the ruins below besides my friends and me. I feel sweetly disoriented, as if I am literally on top of the world. The mountains that surround me feel at once taller and shorter than where I am seated. Condor flies by, silent and undisturbed by our presence. As I sit, a stillness settles within me. I begin to feel the song of the earth vibrate through my bones. In the song I know my life is not meant to fit the norm. I feel possessed with excitement and fear.

The final stop in this vision is of myself about to complete my fourth year at university. I have not graduated but feel too confined by the school system and am trying to decide whether to leave or to try and find a way through. I am plotting my next chapter, and my imagination spills wide. I feel a vertigo of freedom, able to choose whatever I want. I am speaking with my Environmental Psychology professor. He's confusing to my twenty-one-year-old self, as he's a man of great depth and care, passionate about the role our relationship to the earth plays in our well-being, yet he sits across from me in the cafe drinking Coke and smoking cigarettes. He tells me something. Once I hear it, I know it will stick to me. There's no way I can't know. He tells me my desire to go back to Peru, to study and write for a year on the relationship between the earth and the people, is possible. A fabulous idea. He is excited to support me. Never before in my life have I experienced such uncomplicated encouragement. Never before has someone said to my face that my desire, which felt so impossible to me at the time, was not only possible but good. Finding this too confronting, I quit school and move out of state with my boyfriend, initiating a four-year streak of feeling aimless and unmoored.

The three scenes come together to form a triangle, and then all fades to black.

In over twenty years of shamanic work and coaching, I've worked with countless visions, both my own and those of my clients. Because of this, my deeper knowing comes online when these visions arrive.

From this vision, I know every time I see a bird take flight, it's a specific reminder from Spirit that I am here to do the impossible and that my heart is already beating with that which I seek.

I know that the time of the rising sun will continue to gift me medicine and that those movements from darkness into whatever we call light is a place of power for me. I know that I am here for mastery so complete and total that it makes my cells vibrate with aliveness.

I know that mastery for me means that I have gone through the portal myself. I have made the mistakes. I have slogged through the mud and swung through the trees on my way to the goal. Mastery is being willing to go through the whole process of actualization, without squeezing my eyes shut or self-abandoning, so that I can look you in the eyes, unwavering gaze, heart open, and tell you honestly that you can do the same.

I know that I carry within me the capacity to tuck my tail and run as well as the capacity to say yes to myself.

When my circumstances tell me I should say no, I know that my support will often come imperfectly. It will not make sense to me. It will arrive strangely, as an earth psychologist chainsmoker.

I know that support will open me with its completeness of love and championing.

I know that there are dreams yet being born within me, dreams that I have not yet encountered nor seen the faces of. It is to these dreams and to yours that I dedicate this book. The same day of the vision, two clients who had previously said no to committing to high-level work together spontaneously reached out to me and said they were now a yes and wanted to move forward. As I saw birds take flight, I felt courage. I took action on nagging things that I had procrastinated on. Friends I hadn't talked to in months reached out. I felt alive, effortless and in grateful flow.

A CEO once asked me, "When you're talking about manifesting in total ease, you don't mean *no* hard work, do you?"

"Yes I do," I replied.

"Huh," she retorted. "But isn't that just kind of lazy?"

What I shared with her is what I'll share with you now. This fear of being lazy or believing that if you didn't push yourself hard enough to get the flu the victory isn't worth it, is simply control. And control is a trauma response.

Working hard and engaging in self-sacrifice is an evolutionary step. We need to learn how to bend without breaking. What most women don't recognize is that there is a predictable moment when the "hard work" phase is complete and your soul is calling you to grow and give from fullness rather than chronic depletion. When that moment arrives, the learning of hard work is complete. Continuing to live that way breaks you down rather than building you up.

This moment can look like having the life of your dreams but actually feeling empty and unfulfilled. It can look like the reliable practices and tools that in the past have predictably worked to expand you ceasing to be effective. It can sometimes be a harsher wake-up call, like your spouse filing for divorce, receiving a serious diagnosis or learning your child is suicidal.

This spectrum, from a vague sense of boredom to full-fledged crisis, is a call to a greater life.

Look out your window now, or go out onto the land. Find a tree. Notice what you notice and how you notice it. This tree doesn't grow because it's overcoming challenges, earning resources or proving its worth. It grows because it is its nature to grow. And it is the same for you. You are made for abundance, and you are born to manifest. It's not something you learn, it's who you are.

That you are reading this book means that you are entering into this initiation. You are being called to leave the earning, proving, self-sacrifice and self-editing your way to success behind. You are called into a life of deeper magic, mysticism and meaning than you thought possible.

To live a manifested life is the end of codependency. It is the end of scarcity. It is taking full responsibility for your life and reality. Not responsibility as in burden or guilt, but becoming accountable to the power that dwells within you. It is a transcendent way of living where you are no longer trying to please mommy or daddy, or whatever you have projected mommy or daddy onto. You no longer seek self-worth and belonging by fitting into any sort of outer narrative. You live by your own law.

Without conscious participation in your own evolution, you remain disempowered. If you do not empower yourself intellectually, you'll be told what to do. If you don't empower yourself financially, you'll be told what you're worth. If you don't empower your decision, others will make your choices. Disempowerment is not something that happens to us from outside, it is a choice we make. And the moment you choose to empower yourself by living a manifested life, everything will change.

To make this shift requires a map. This book offers that map. It is a shamanic navigational tool that will awaken your native virtue and support you in self-liberation and inner authority. It will give you access to living a manifested life, one filled with abundance, magic and power.

This book is the distillation of my twenty years of work in shamanic practice and actualization. My work centers on The Wheel. You may have heard of The Medicine Wheel, a term that loosely refers to the circular map of meaning and relationship found in multiple North and South American indigenous traditions. The Wheel is often understood to have four directions, like a compass. Each of these directions is associated with a different energy, for instance the seasons or the phases of the moon. Sometimes the directions are associated with different animal spirit allies. The Wheel gives us a sense of the potential power and pitfall each of these energies holds, as well as the potential relationship between them. The Wheel is also a sacred metaphor for the evolution and maturation of human beings.

What most people don't realize is that The Wheel is not an esoteric practice that exclusively belongs to Native American cultures. It is present, in some form, in all human traditions that have ancient roots. We have the Celtic Wheel of the Seasons as well as the Ayurvedic Seasonal Wheel. Tibetan Buddhism has a Wheel called The Five Buddha Families. Even Christianity's liturgical calendar happens on a wheel that relates to the seasons and lunar cycles. The Wheel does not belong to any one culture but is a human tool. To work with it is to touch on something intrinsic to human mysticism, development and meaning.

The first season of my own work was in shamanic ayurveda and Jungian dreamwork. I discovered a wheel at that time created by Toni Wolff, a partner to Jung in his work. She devoted herself to working with the anima, the feminine aspects in a woman's psyche. She identified four core archetypes, or energetic principles, that are at play for all women throughout their lives.

The hetaira, held in the south of her wheel, is like a Geisha. She is sexy, a muse. She is our sensual aspect.

In the west of this wheel we find the mystic. The deeply magical, intuitive and oracular nature all women carry.

In the north we find the mother archetype. We know ourselves to be the source of life here and feel accountable to creation as an expression of ourselves.

Finally in the East we have the amazon. The boss bitch. This is our capacity to be out in patriarchy and to remould it to our own design.

Each archetype holds vast potential and also tremendous shadow. Each archetype relates to the others.

The most interesting aspect of this Wheel is how a woman navigates embodying these archetypes. In the broadest strokes, women usually have one archetype that feels most like a "home base"—the archetype they most easily embody. As women begin to embody more of themselves, they will feel drawn to encompass additional archetypes, usually moving around the Wheel in a circle.

The most potent transformational moments on a woman's journey happen when she moves straight across, for instance when she is identified with the witchy mystic and seeks to also fully embody her boss bitch self, without compromising either. Wolff named this sort of transit as both the most challenging and the most rewarding.

In my own decades of work, I've brought the archetypes into my dreams. The poetry expressed in this book is sourced directly from my nighttime dreams and vibrates with the frequency of each of these archetypes. Connecting with the poems awakens and activates the dormant potential held within you. As these energies flow more powerfully through you, your impact, joy, revenue and power increase.

Through these years of work, my own Wheel has emerged. Informed by the many Wheels I have worked with, this Wheel deals specifically with the energetic architecture required to manifest a life of your dreams. I discovered through working with thousands of women that these four core archetypes are brought to consciousness through a specific frequency.

Decision activates the hetaira. In this section you'll learn how to access deep pleasure and literally create anything you want by clarifying your *yes* and your *no*.

Surrender illuminates the indwelling mystic. Here we'll explore the magic and ecstasy available in losing control.

Inspired action brings power to our inner mother. We feel at our best when we embody the full ownership of our process. This section will illuminate how this happens.

Receiving opens the portals of expression for the amazon. To have what you want is to liberate yourself from scarcity. Receiving is a radical practice that changes not only your life but the lives of those around you.

The stage is set for us to begin with desire. Desire is at the center of the Wheel. It is the hub around which our entire life emerges and to which it returns. Saying yes to desire is the first step in living an empowered, manifested and abundant life.

CHAPTER 1

Desire: Offer You for the Destiny of All

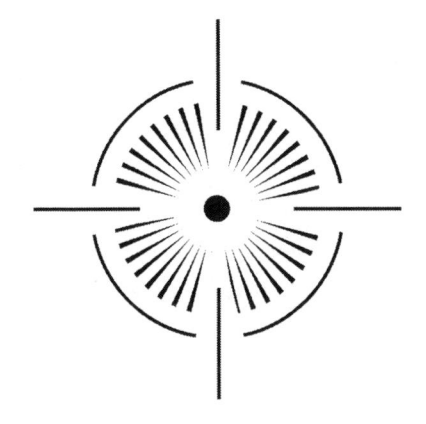

Rub paste in my eyes
The grit of stars carving a new vision
Dance me in your crazy ways
Paint your signs on my skin

How would you live if you knew that your desire, when fully trusted and followed, would always lead to the highest good?

You might embark on a new career, or speak shocking truths from the deep wells of love within you. You might start a cult or lead a revolution. You might walk away. You might choose to stay. You might leave your lover or take a new one. You might invent a completely new modality of healing, write a book that changes the world, amass wealth or simply begin your day in a ritual of self-massage with warm and spiced oils. Though desire is a universal experience, the way it moves in each of us is as unique as a fingerprint.

The shape of your desire is your true destiny. The ancient Upanishad texts of the Vedic tradition advise, "As your deepest driving desire is, so shall your life be." Living in an unedited *yes* to your desire opens previously invisible portals of pleasure, connection, magic and opportunity. When freed of fear and shame conditioning, your desire allows the flow of the best of you. It is the path of authenticity so many women are searching for but are unable to consciously embody.

How do you fully trust and follow your desire? In this moment, bring your energy all the way down into your toes. Without moving them, simply sense their shape and place. Feel the space between them. They may even seem invisible—this is perfect. Simply keep pressing towards them with your attention. Let them grab you with the innocence that a child grabs her mother's hand. With your attention still there, let your breath begin to stretch and broaden through you. Now open. Turn towards. Listen, as if in dream. Let your toes express themselves to you. Ask them, "What do you want? What would you love to do?" Receive the answer. Even if it is silence, receive it. Even if it is the slightest warmth spreading. And then act on it, now. The true flavor of your desire unfurls freely and clearly in this kind of intimacy.

When fear, scarcity and shame shroud desire, something very different happens. Severed from an intimacy with desire, most people are immature and unripened within it. This immaturity expresses as an unwillingness to feel desire or to open to the destiny lines it's calling us towards. Desire deteriorates into compulsion and addiction, unconsciously identified with and acted out. Or it manifests as a control response to life, your heart moving back with shoulders rounded as you we shrink away from your inner life and replace it with what seems acceptable, palatable and pleasing to those around you.. You become restless, constantly not wanting to be where you are.

There is no escape from desire. It is the center of the Wheel of Manifestation. It is where all is born from and returns to. Most high-achieving women are still living a script that outlines endless cycles of forcing and exhaustion with a yearning for freedom and flow that they only half believe are possible. But you didn't come here to expertly live out someone else's narrative. You came here to forge a new path. That path is found in fostering such a radical kinship with desire that you can feel its true voice in your pulse and you give yourself everything that you want, immediately, without weighing pros and cons. Genuine care and thoughtfulness have nothing to do with trying to assess how others will metabolize your choices and then conforming to what you think will rock the boat the least. This is a confusion between real harm and impact. It is codependency and control with a mask of false concern. Attempting to control the lives of others by never causing provocation may give you a temporary feeling of safety, but it is only creating a powder keg of unlived life that will either explode your relationships or implode you. Genuine love is living in transparency. It is taking the risk of being hated for what you are versus being loved for what you are not.

When "failures" happen, they are a wake-up call for the call to this greater authenticity. Your business launch flopping, getting the flu for the third time this year or waking up to find your marriage has become an emptiness need not be a cause to immediately search for what you or someone else did "wrong." They can be recognized as life stripping you of barriers you've erected between yourself and your desire. Rather than obsessively trying to fix yourself, you can simply ask, "What am I not giving myself that I really want?" Having the courage to ask, receive the answer and take action can turn your dark nights of the soul into beacons of light that have you shining open like the sun.

Our individual paths all lead to this essential truth: you are always living desire. You are either living your own or someone else's. You will either live it consciously, which liberates you into flow, power and aliveness, or you will live it unconsciously, meeting life with a constant cringe. You have been waiting, hoping, wishing for the moment when it will be safe to live as who you actually are. Waiting for some elusive guarantee that if you were to stop pretending, you would still be loved. But waiting is always suffering. Waiting is withholding.

You do not need to wait. You can choose, right now, to remember that you are love. Because you are love, your desires are love. Withholding your desire is withholding your love. And when your unlived life accumulates within you, your guarantee is that your life will be a wasteland. This moment, right now, you can prioritize your desire. You can fall open to it. You can listen for the cascade of sensation-language it is speaking to you. You can care about what turns you on and reject anything that doesn't.

If familiar fear, shame and judgment surface, don't try to fix them or get rid of them. Feel them fully. Don't believe them. Don't identify with them. Go in. Go into the hot fist of contraction your stomach becomes. Feel the closure and dryness of your throat, the shallow sadness of your breath. Feel the grip of your cervix as you choose this fear yet again. Feel how you've bartered your life to its hold. Fall open to it.

Keep doing this. Keep opening. Nothing else to do. Watch as it dismantles itself and disappears completely. See how it does this because you stopped running and turned towards it. Find your life again. Let your feet fall heavier on the earth until your hip creases soften. Gift yourself with breath. Let this breath comb through you, removing any residual tangles. Notice where your attention goes. Feel the shape of your desire bringing its warm intelligence to soften your belly, to buoy your heart.

Know that this will happen again and again. Your desire will show you the greater life that is possible. You will explore moving towards it. Fear, shame and contraction will surface. What is different now is that you know there's no meaning you need to assign to any of it. And there's nothing you need to do, overcome, fix or change. There is only choosing to stay here, choosing to feel, not turning away. Fear will rise and it will fall, but it can no longer convince you to turn away from your desire. No part of you will be scapegoated again.

The destiny, ground, purpose and connection we seek can only be lived by saying yes to desire. And further, following it in the deeply personal, creative and surprising ways that we only become aware of in the moment. Expressing your deepest love to your children isn't in the premeditated and highly orchestrated events. It is found in the ways you softly brush the hair out of your child's eyes when she reveals she's afraid. In business, high-level, ten-out-of-ten clients are not created by clever marketing but by speaking the truth you see, the truth you *want* to speak, the truth that most people would never dare to speak. The authentic embodiment of our desire happens thousands of ways. Its unique expression is only found in this moment.

Desire is an alchemy, constantly expanding the edges of your life. Whatever joy you've felt, you can access greater joy. Whatever connection and understanding you've known is infinitely multiplied. The accomplishment that seems so far off and exhausting now becomes immediately and easily accessible.

Desire will challenge you. Both because it will mean transformation into more genuineness and power when you follow it, and also because the societal conditioning you carry is literally anchored into your tissues. They will complain as you expand. But as you literally move your bodies to follow where desire leads, in honoring and faith, desire becomes like a liniment to the achy places where your identity is beginning to stretch and roar.

POEMS OF DESIRE

1.

May the warmth of my altar
Weave through all realms
May the heart of my heart
Yearn and stretch with all others
May this prayer
Dizzy us with all
That is possible

2.

I accept your discomfort with my untethered want
My breath bated with a yearning
I want everything
I want money and sex
I want the shocking green of my cat's eyes
I want love to be more than a platitude
I want it to be more than a silly plaque accenting a wall
Live
Laugh
Love
I want the order of our lives to be inflected with so much laughter that our bellies ache and our faces hurt with it
I want it to shake us into a heap on the earth
I want to live so hard I collapse each night into a slumber still rich with the smell of warm grass in my nostrils
With stars in my hair and mud between my toes
I want a love so outrageous that it reveals
every dream and causes me to live it
Without hiding behind health insurance
or what will my mother think
I want no more indigenous women disappeared
I want women to have money and power
To sink their teeth in and let the juices run down their cheeks where tears of despair fell days before
I want us to suckle every moment of this life for the blessing that it is, singular, unrepeatable, no matter whether bitter or salty or sweet.
I want nothing
I want the void
I want the dizzy expanse of cliff edges

that turn my brain inside out with the openness
I want the null, the negative, the unseen
I want things undone and unclaimed
I am free in my wanting as it is the birthing point of change
I am free in my wanting because yes or no is not the point
The point is to feel full with insatiability
To remove the hand over my mouth and sing a song of deep longing
And ceaseless crave

3.

Don't wait until you are ready
In fact, don't wait
At all
Ever
While you wait, something is wasting
The ripeness of this moment
The perfect tendrils of nourishment that scrape and crawl across the lens of your awareness
The drops
That you were waiting to arrive, bottled and labeled for easy interpretation
Don't wait
You can trust this moment
See how it opens itself to you, naked, scented, rich, generous
No more holding back
No more hiding behind polite forbearance
The time is now
Don't hold back
Offer the rich imperfection
The bounty
Of you

4.

What happens in these moments?
These moments of more of less
That grow deeper and wider with each breath.
This breath, a shape that Spirit makes
When It touches the body.
A shape of softening
That widens us to touch
The realm of grief and hope
That opens toward us now.
To spill fingers over its sharp and surprising
Edge.
Who do we become now?
With so much changed,
Some still moored, stuck, untouched.
A contracted form, voice tight.
Fighting the way we always fought.
Willing for or against, like always.
And yet, something bright and lit
And strange stirs within.
Now is the shape of something new.
New breath, breathing a new people.
New purpose, a purpose lived
Not held in concepts.
Sourced in our tissues
In our belonging
To blood and bone
To the clay earth and sweet grass
To each other.
A purpose needing no understanding
Only to make its shape
Of love.

5.

You carry it with you wherever you go
I will not be the first to say this
But I open my throat in the hope that hearing it
through my voice will call forward your own.
Something is brewing.
A voice. A hunger. A gift.
This is how the story goes.

6.

Destiny Song

I did not come here to live my life by standards of capitalist achievement or tidy accolades.

I came here to measure my life by how fully I devote to giving and receiving in each moment.

I didn't come to be neat, orderly and compliant.

I seek no balance but relish the poignant tension it brings that absolves and dissolves and clarifies all that has been with all that has yet to be.

I didn't come here to please you, but to see deep into all that you are from all that I am.

I didn't incarnate to play it safe.

I came here to serve and disrupt.

I came here to feel how past and future press themselves into my brain just now, to notice their presence and how it gives shape and texture to things.

I came here to see and smell and listen deep. I came to feel and fuck and moan and scream and whisper and laugh. I came here to love my animal body.

I came here to feel the blade edges of life, leaning into pain and pleasure so fully that I find the convergence of where they are no longer different.

I came here to awaken and to sing to what wakes in you.

We are not different.

I came here to create sanctuary, to sink my teeth into duality and trouble so that I can problem solve and learn and recover the ancient voices that sing in me.

I came here to know myself as Ancestor. To remember that all that I am is borrowed and not my own and at the same time so unique as to never be repeated again. I came here to perk my ears, to make big mistakes, to learn how to tell a truth so powerful that the only thing ever to cross my lips is the flavor of love.

I came here to create a refuge for the shadow, for all that we have disavowed. I am shepherdess of darkness and midwife of light. I came here to bridge, like a song that needs somewhere to go, some new harmony or cadence or arc. I came here to bridge like what we accept now and what has yet to find a place in our knowing.

I came here to mother. To be the one who honors the spirits that incarnated through my body. I came here to mend the legacy as best I can that there is more space inside of them for what is truly of them, for it is truly a thing of beauty.

I didn't come here to behave. The code in my bones doesn't know how. The blood in my womb has something different in mind. I came here to call the soul pieces home, to serve your wholeness and mine and to give something sacred back to the spirit of the Earth. I came to give back to the Earth what is Hers.

I came here to initiate, to absolve us of all the trauma and spin it into gold. To return it back to its natural habitat of wisdom.

I came to facilitate what is wild and cunning and present and filled with stars and unto itself that thing that still exists, yes, in each and every one.

I came here to remember well, and to be remembered well.

7.

Listen for the voice of truth.

Listen for its heartbeat at the deep center of your life.

Feel it move as earthworms move in the soil organism beneath your feet. Feel it as the robins do, knowing the precise location—the wiggle and circumnavigation of every intrepid insect.

The voice of truth is ever-changing. And it changes you. If it does not change you, it is not the truth. It is a shapeshifter, as the *curanderos*, the *curanderas* of the jungles and Apus that speak only to them. There is a way of knowing, they say, when you taste the blood in your mouth as Jaguar. That way of knowing is beyond reach when you walk the way a human walks. When you are human, death stalks you. Jaguar stalks death. Become the shapeshifter.

We have this story of how love is kept from us, how life has wronged us, how we've been sanctioned. Truth says, "It's never been about the Universe opening a door when another closes. It's *you* that needs to open the door, *you* that needs to dispense the blessing, to allow love to walk through with the codes of the cosmos imprinted on the backs of its hands, the gifts of belonging held in its leathery old palms." Truth says, "It's exhausting, you know, living a life that's not your own."

Truth reincarnates, a star imploding on itself only to be born again. Same breath, new form. No inhale, no exhale, ever alike, ever the same. I invited my client, a woman I have the privilege to sit with, the other day, "Go to your mirror for ten minutes nonstop. Trace every line on your blessed face. Love the shape of every bone. Notice what changes." She says the light has come back to her eyes. You can see it. Truth is like this. My client is truth, and so are you and so am I. And it's nothing to mourn that we're so fucking forgetful. It's in the untethering of our knowing that the electric seeds of re-membering find anchor for their technicolor roots.

The Sky Nation has had a lot of conversation around this lately. The Sun, that radiant Masculine portal, burst through the clouds to call me into place for ceremony. Manifested a rainbow, a *cuichi*, when no rain had announced its arrival or ushered its departure. It blessed our sacred arrangement. When we sat in sacred circle, everyone came in with heavy hearts, the clouds crowding ominously. As we swept the space of our hearts with breath, the sky opened and dappled its praise on our grateful faces. And as I sat with another client, in our ceremony tears began to roll over her lashes, suddenly. What are they about? Why did they arrive? At the same moment, the sky cried with her. The forecast had not called for anything but partial sun. Where did this sudden burst of rain come from and why? It lasted only a few minutes. The rain came for her. The Sky Nation wept with her. This is truth.

So many sweet souls, so many of my human comrades, I hear lamenting, "This change is never-ending! What shall we ever do!?! I don't want to change my paradigm! I just found furniture for this one!" And with all the gentleness my heart can hold on its shores I respond. If I was ever going to speak prophecy, it would be this: The cycles of accelerated change are not going anywhere. This is the life we said yes to when we hitched a ride in these skin containers. This experience of the universe falling apart and then putting itself back together in the space of an afternoon (or less time, actually) is simply the nature of things. It has always been. It's just now we are able to tolerate the light thrown off by this Wheel. Now we are able to see as Jaguar sees.

To see deep.

To see all the way through.

This is no death sentence. This is no punishment. This is no drama.

This is freedom. It tastes like blood in your mouth the way the river is the blood of the earth tasted by the Sea when river empties itself to Her. Sometimes pain, but no harm. Sadness, joy, anger; all can move free of threads of attachment. It is the blood of finally spitting out all that venom, all the tasteless days, all the ways you've played along, all the ways you've put your bet on the long-gone past. Even the change-aholics do it.

Truth is speaking. It's easy to hear once you don't need it to confirm your identity or belief. Once you don't need it to justify your existence. It's easy to hear when you don't expect it to sound any particular way or adhere to some script or scripture.

Truth melts in your mouth like sunlight in the air, like salt impregnates the waters of ocean and tears. Form surrendering itself for the greater cause of receptivity.

My Tracking Jaguar told me her name: Matangi. I was also told by the elders that my tracking Jaguar ought to be male, but Mantangi doesn't care. Sometimes she is a she and sometimes he is a he. The name, Matangi, sounded familiar but I have not known why. She is black and gleaming, with a *cuichi* always right above her head, often with blood dripping from her mouth, like Kali. Yes, like Kali, when you gaze deep into her ferociousness, all you find is a well of compassion.

I learned recently that Matangi was the name of an ancient forest Goddess in India. She is the outcast, the muse, the keeper of plant medicine knowledge. She holds the wisdom of knowing that the ways we perceive ourselves as different from others are not a problem, as we may assume them to be. As we allow "otherness" to become part of the beautiful and ever-changing weave of self, we find an initiation into partnership and belonging.

Aha!

8.

There is a path to your destiny
That is totally unpredictable
It does not depend on circumstance
Or opinion
It only depends on your commitment
To being who you are
To being the love, the care, the light
That you are
Keep the sun at your back
My friend

9.

In the garden of my heart, flowers of peace bloom beautifully.
Peace is not outside of me, but within me.
When I make dedicated space for my heart,
in my language,
in my schedule,
in my breath,
in my vision,
Peace prevails.
Be more in love with your future today
Than with the suffering of the past
Remember who you are
When a smile has lived
Across the distance
Of your heart
Remember the joy
Of health and hearty laughter
Hear the voices
Of love
From the future
Let it draw you out
Of tired and defensive shapes
Let the memory of the future
Open your limitless loving heart
Now
The fire I tend
Is the cauldron
Of promise.
Hope is the balm of winter
That softens what had hardened

In the glare of summer sun.
Solitude, rest and reflection
Open me to the support
That has always been there,
Allowing for fresh resolve
And deeper heart.
What will end with me today?
What begins with me today?

10.

It's not your massive business experience
Or even your brilliant mind—
It can solve any problem!
But it's not that
It's not funding
Or popularity
It's because you are
A woman with a heart
A heart that holds
The whole
A heart
That speaks
A deeper truth
This is why you
Are the hope
Of all of us
This is why we choose you
And why you
Are the one
We follow
You hold our hearts
In your heart
We hold your heart
In ours

11.

You deserve spaces saturated by gratitude, respect and cooperation.

These are the high-quality nourishments your soul requires.

Love yourself enough to create and say yes to these generative spaces. Don't starve your soul!

Depression is only this: the *deep rest* that the body requires, because it is exhausted by holding up an identity. Take rest. Nourish your soul. When you do this, everything will change.

12.

You are a manifestation of the One.
You are whole and holy.
You are the truth.
My invitation today is that in any moment where you judge yourself, or worry others are judging you,
That is the place where you bless, celebrate, forgive and love.
This is the fastest way to transform consciousness

13.

Everywhere I go
It's you I search for
I think I'm looking for socks
But it's you I want to feel under my feet
Everywhere I go
It's your face I see
Look at me
See me
No
Don't just see me
Feel me
Hear me
Touch me
Understand me
Hold me
Smell me
Embrace me
You pulled the veil back
And showed me that
Place
Where all the smoke and mirrors fade
A nothing so dense
It is
Everything
"It is done," you said
The search is over
This is the gold at the end
Of the rainbow
Everything I thought I wanted
To create

To build
To destroy
Was you
Now I only search for you
We play hide and seek
Lost and
Finally
Found

14.

Woman is mystery
Woman is magic
Woman is love
Woman is rhythm
Woman is blood, is power, is ache, is longing, is fulfillment
Woman,
Meet your power
Practice your power
Be your power
Eat from the center
Play with your power
Play the game of being the Divine
incarnate
You are your power when you are not you
But when you are YOU
The One Goddess
10,000 forms
Laughter goddess
Crying goddess
Shitting goddess
Bleeding goddess
Singing goddess
Mothering goddess
Sensing goddess
I choose you
You carry The Power
In your mouth,
Delicate,
Between your teeth
Smiling, true

Your throat burns
And I make medicine for you
Pouring the sweet elixir
Down your tortured throat
Soothing
Soma
Hurt is the secret
Essential ingredient
Of healing
No hurt, no need to heal
It comes from the place
Where I would never go
You hold it for me
You carry it in your throat
When I forget who I am
the power that I am
I retrieve from the center
When I remember
I retrieve it from within

15.

I am another yourself
Every cell
A portal
Of remembering
Of intimate-ing
That heartbreak was never mine
Borrowed only
From the ancient, deep folds
Like a wrinkle in the old skin
Of time
Surrendering the hard edges of the heart
My hands and mouth
Soften
Once again
Surrendering the ragged voice
Of hurt
I receive you now
Taste you now
Now I eat you
Now you eat me
Unencumbered feast of love
Innocent
Open
Hunger
Satisfaction blurring
The lines
Of separateness
Devouring me
Into
Wholeness

16.

The human condition comes with a yen to end the trance of separation and have a lived experience of belonging.

As we reach for this experience, in our relationships, communities and within ourselves, our tendencies train our vision, our bodies and our breath.

We habitually seek belonging by finding others like us.

Often sameness is so wired with belonging that we mistakenly believe it is a requirement.

In times when pressures and stress rise, the yearning for belonging can become so great that we deny there is any difference at all.

We don't share what's inside of us, for fear of the distance it might create.

In the same way, we deny how others' experience,
views or values might differ from our own in an attempt to keep the bond intact.

We feel that to be different
might burn the bridge between us.

This becomes problematic, though, doesn't it?

Rather than anxious scanning and assessing for how I might
be different or same with the life within me and around me, I can soften my
gaze, let my peripheral vision come online
see something new.

I can see that belonging is not the result of sameness.

Belonging is the experience of something shared.

17.

Knowing there's no land called "when this is all over" that we can find
What will you choose to look for?
Knowing that there's no going back
What the deepest yearning in your heart?
What are you seeking that is
Seeking you?
When we lose a limb, we can wait
And wait until our last breath
For it to grow back.
Waiting for a day that will never come
Waiting for a permission we never needed.
Or
we can feel what life is like now,
What grows in that space that's been freed up
By all the things that have died off and will not return.
We can turn the stones in our hearts and joints over
To see the new life
Growing, sprouting recklessly, wildly
Beneath the weight.

18.

My eyes are on fire
With visions of you
Like smoke stings
Every form a spark
A display
Of your dance

19.

You are worth remembering
You are worth kindness
In all your growth and passion
You are worthy of gentleness
Holy temple woman
Holy temple man
Holy temple human
Holy temple beings
I see you
I honor you

20.

I used to serve from wanting
To be filled up
Wanting the assurance that
If I make you
Happy
Healed
Better
Then I know I exist
Know I am okay
Then once I knew I existed
I served wanting safety
Of exchange.
"If I serve, the universe will respond.
I'll have enough. If I just do enough right things something will come back."
Now I set my service free
I serve because I understand
Feeling fear is just calling me to serve
Not serving so that I don't fear
But fear as a green light at the intersection of my energy
When I feel fear, I laugh a little
I know it's just time to
Reach out, love expand
Serve

21.

No need to always be upbeat
No downbeat, no rhythm
No rhythm, no dance
I'm reaching now
Up and down and inside out
Breathing in and out of
My full range
All my dimensions
No fear of darkness
No hiding my light
Letting it all in
Breathing it all out

22.

The good is written in my heart
The wings of the morning
I am the temple where god dwells
Every night I wrap myself in the blanket of the stars' love
I cast my burdens off into the hands of spirit
The rhythm of god finds itself in me
Lips parted
Exhale

DESIRE RITUAL

To move from the desire-center of the Wheel and into the next dream, the dream of decision, I offer you a ritual. Ritual moves us beyond psychology and physicality and into the energetic.

Before you proceed, pause with me.

Notice, do you desire to go into this ritual?

Please, take a risk with me in this container. Only proceed if you really want to. Feel free to take only what you want and leave anything you don't. Do you want to be in this ritual with me?

If your desire is moving you towards this ritual, follow the QR code to receive my guidance. We'll weave in the journal prompts below.

(ritual - a desire journal, practicing with the earth)

JOURNAL PROMPTS FOR DESIRE

What would I do, say or be if there were no repercussions?

When have I lived my desire so fully that everything changed?

When I consider taking the risk of living my desire fully, what do I come up against?

What helps me to remain open in my desire?

What closes me off?

Who can support me in living my desire fully?

How have I tried to protect others, or myself, by rejecting my desire?

Whose desires am I living out when I am not living my own?

What do I believe I have to gain by controlling and suppressing desire?

What are the costs of this?

What is the potential for me in exploring living in my desire consciously?

What will happen if I continue to live out the current patterns?

What am I willing to shift within myself to allow my desire to take me all the way to my destiny?

CHAPTER 2

Decision: Let Your Destiny Live

Deep Power
Isn't interested in safety
Its purpose is meant to frighten us
Out
Of stagnation
Pull us apart into
Deeper chambers of love
Dangle us
Above destinies that shine

Your deepest gifts are expressed most profoundly through your choice. Your *yes* and your *no* are the mechanisms through which your greatest authenticity is expressed. The deeper and clearer your choice, the more you are drenched in love and blessing. The more you embody your decision, the more your life is transformed by truth. When you fail to embody decision, your deepest gifts go completely unlived, ungiven and unreceived.

Don't wait. Begin your embodiment now. Give your gifts. Open. Completely receive the gifts being offered to you. Recognize the gift of life in all its forms. Feel anger as gift. When you express your disappointment to another, be clear that you are gifting them. When miracles occur, be fully expressed inside of them. Allow yourself to squeal out loud with delight and dance wildly in public, feeling how you are blessing those around you.

Love is not generic. It blooms in you differently than it does in anyone else. When someone you know is sick, your love might move toward them in the form of delivering chicken soup. But for another it would be giving advice. For yet another it might be doing nothing. The way you are made to love is your destiny. It is your path to abundance as well as the destination. Your way can only be discovered in this moment. It is a spontaneous experience born of the alchemy of the moment and your presence within it. Desire opens the portal to destiny. Decision is what gives us ground to anchor our destiny into.

You know what you want and what you don't. But that internal clarity is obscured in your daily life, replaced with anxiety, overwhelm and internal conflict. These experiences create a near-constant internal pressure within leader-women. Whether you experience this in small doses, at the margins of your consciousness or as the overarching theme of your day, this pressure, when left unmet and unattended, quickly leads to a life that is too small for you, void of aliveness and authenticity. You want to experience the delight of money flowing easily and plentifully through your business, but you spend all day stressing about your revenue and denying your true expression while doing what you think you "have to" do in order to grow your wealth. Or you exhaust yourself by trying to be a "good mom" at the expense of your own health and the depth of your other relationships. At other times you may be aching for sensuality, deep love-making and all kinds of bright, unbounded pleasure, but you move through your days depressed and dampened by the waves of lack you feel hitting the shores of your life.

Come into your throat. Right now. Feel the subtle cascade of sensation as you draw breath through your throat and release from it. Don't try to relax. Simply witness. Staying with the throat, bring to mind a circumstance in your life where you feel a "have to." Notice what changes, if anything. Map the impact of all that pressure on this sacred space of throat. What do you find when you look there? Sense tightness. Turn towards constraint. Hold space for heat. Now drop your attention to your womb-space. Even if your womb has been removed, its energy and intelligence remain. The echo of "have to" lives here as well, tissues closed off, clenched or vacant.

The absence of empowered, authentic decision is the deep root of this dissonance. Tissues gripping is a physical expression of a life of withholding. Your withholding is the echo of wisdom, not fault. There was a moment in your life when the joy of giving your deepest gifts threatened something deeply important. Perhaps the love of a parent would be withheld if you "acted out" and were too silly or loud or wouldn't be still. Even the threat of losing our parents' love is often enough to trigger a pattern of internal gripping. You are no longer a child. This pattern of contraction is not keeping you safe or guaranteeing love. Without clear choice, you feel life is always coming at you rather than unfurling from within you.

Inevitably, you learned along the way to take others' desires on as your own. You became what you believed you needed to be in order to receive love, dignity, affirmation and ground. This sets the foundation for living in trade-offs. You operate inside of a belief structure that to choose one thing of value means we must sacrifice an essential piece of self.

Inside of this paradigm, making a clear choice starts to feel like it leads to less. If I say yes to charging soul-aligned rates, my clients will desert me. If I assert my truth, I'll compromise the peace in our family.

Sensing that decision leads to loss and not gain, we protect ourselves by going unconscious inside of it. We distract ourselves with packed schedules, social media or personal drama. When our desire asserts itself, we use complaint and blame to avoid having to make a clear and empowered choice. I can't count the number of sales calls I've been in where the applicant wants to point to money, time, her spouse, her past, anything other than herself as the reason why she can or cannot move forward. I've also seen women hide inside of a trance of indecision, hoping and wishing with fingers crossed that something or someone will make the decision for them. A sign will come, or certainty or confidence will arrive and then somehow they'll know. Without embodying decision, our life persists in fantasy.

The result of projecting the power of our decision onto our circumstances or hiding from it is that we build the house of our lives on unstable ground. In my first marriage, I spent the better part of a year agonizing over whether to stay or go. During those months I had a recurring dream. In every version of this dream, I was trying to get into my house. I was always greeted by an old woman who evoked the quintessential blend of fairy godmother and midwestern grandma. She was plump and short with short, gray, permed hair. Always she wore baggy mom jeans and a sweatshirt with appliqués. And every single time I tried to get into the house, she'd slam the door in my face.

I was seeking refuge in a space that could not provide it. I was waiting for clarity, for just a little more information, for a sign from God. What I didn't realize then is that I had the equation backwards. I thought I needed clarity in order to decide. The truth is, decision is what provides clarity.

We feel at our best when we own our life. In order to own our life, we must take the risk of choosing it. A magnificent life doesn't happen by chance. It happens by decision.

You can experience decision as a path of more and not less. The bliss of decision can begin here and now. Bring your womb and throat into your attention once again. These are the two energy centers from which we give and also into which we receive. They vibrate with the wisdom of our deepest yes and no. Allow the fullness of your desire to fill you. Bring it into your body and your breath with sweet specificity. What do you really want? And as you open fully to desire, how do these sacred centers in your body express? Can you feel warmth? Tingling, spreading waves rippling?

Once you can feel the energy of desire, consider something you believe you will have to sacrifice or trade if you were to have that desire fulfilled. Perhaps you believe you can generate a certain amount of revenue, but not in the span of time you'd really love. Or maybe you look wistfully out your window every day, just wishing you could go for a long, exploratory hike. You want to move your body. You know the stiffness and pain in your joints isn't just "aging." It's your body crying for a healthier routine. But you "have to" get these emails out, this page built, etc. because if you don't, no one will buy from you. Or you believe to keep harmony in your marriage, there are certain aspects of your depth that must remain out of sight to your beloved.

Feel the contrast in your body. Find its nexus. The next step is where the magical alchemy of decision becomes known. I want you to choose that these two things that seem not to go together, must. That you will have the money you want arrive in your bank account in the time span that is correct for you. That you can have all the clients you want and still go on a hike every day, taking as long as you like to satisfy your curiosity and saturate your senses with the scent of sap, the crunch of trail gravel beneath your feet and the kiss of gentle breezes on your skin. That you can show every side of you to your lover and they will not reject you.

This decision may not make sense to you at first. This is only because you are beginning to create masterfully with the unknown. Nothing new can happen in the known. This disorientation is only the feeling of more. Though it may feel unfamiliar and strange, it is ground beginning to gather beneath you.

In order to embody this decision and bring it out of fantasy and into full-fledged vision, surrender to that-which-is-greater is required. The sacred interconnectivity between decision and surrender alchemize a promise of manifesting a life beyond what you can imagine.

Every act of decision is an offering. We can feel it in our bodies when someone is saying yes to themselves in the deepest degree of truth. It arrives as gift. It moves like lightning through our cells, causing jaw to drop, laughter to emerge and even a victory cry with fists raised. Do not reduce yourself by being agreeable. Do not be convinced by anything other than the voice of your own soul.

What you decide is what you have. What you decide is what you become. Everything you think you cannot have, cannot be, cannot do is accessed through choosing it. Knowing your desire is not all that useful. Feeling it can be profound. Choosing your desire is what transforms your life.

POEMS OF DECISION

1.

A constant invitation
An open secret
Birth is death
Death is birth
What are you waiting for?
You have permission

2.

I've come a long way to tell this story.
Bridges burned and doors shut.
The past will no longer be something to point to
For who you are and what you choose.
The radiant Sun is a life-giver
Who shows up without fail.
And what do we do with all this precious energy?
Limbs of Source
Become the Solar King, the Solar Queen
We came here to be.
You are on time.
It's time to take your place
In Munay-Ki, to be
Love In Action.

3.

Eye of Mother

Standing across waters
Earth and Air am I
Fire and Spirit am I
Standing across waters
Distances close
Oneness only
Standing across waters
My gaze untethered and wild
Splintered shards of me
Puzzling back together
A heart come home
Is there anything I can't know here?
What ends with me, now?
What begins with me, now?
Edge of sky tongues those waves
Her shimmer-dance a slick lick
Imprinting air with her peaks and valleys
Life devouring itself back into love
Suddenly
Every no
Never said spills over my teeth
Every yes I swallowed
Hisses and spits like fire
Ecstatic dance on my lips
No more maybe
Or just wait
Or until

Or what if
Now
Here
This
Life underscored
So many times
Shouting in my ears
Pounding in my throat
I stuck my fingers in my ears
Lalalalala
Now I open, open, open
Now I am crossroads
I am threshold
I am bridge
Fingering opposites
Fierce, light, free
This moment
Standing across waters
A deeper wholeness
A mystery weave
Dances on the grave
Of who I was
Now I carve my path
With no and yes
Silent and certain
Like oar in water
Like wind horse
Like your hand inside
my heart
And mine inside yours

4.

Does it matter what others think?
There's a place
A part of you so deep,
So untouched.
This place is the Void of you
Your fear and fascination.
It's the white-hot power of you,
That drowns when there are too many other irons in the fire.
It's the terrible ancient ache with you, the secret sanctum of your heart
And your blood
the place that yearns to be seen, tasted, honored
It's the yearning to be held more completely than you've ever known
And to create, free of the tethers and leashes of conventional living.

5.

You have permission.
You have permission to bring the lightning down.
You have permission to feel.
You have permission to change your mind.
You have permission to be tired.
You have permission to not be perfect.
You have permission to say no.
You have permission to say yes when your heart agrees to it.
You have permission to have a dirty house.
You have permission to wake with a smile.
You have permission to thunder.
You have permission to let it all out.
You have permission to stay.
You have permission to be angry.
You have permission to spread your wings wide, picking up the vibration.
You have permission to be uncertain.
You have permission to grieve.
You have permission to be awkward.
You have permission to take all the time you need.
You have permission to walk away from all that you worked for, if it no longer reflects your soul's longing.
You have permission to voice.
You have permission to create.
You have permission to shine.
You have permission to be imbalanced, to be not-calm and to be disorganized.
You have permission to BE.

6.

You are loved through all moments, not just the ones where you are well-behaved. Primordial energy and vitality are restored not through caffeine, good self-care, or eating clean. Love alone restores. Love yourself radically enough that you feel totally acceptable. Let love tear down those unyielding walls, brick by brick. Wholeness is restored by the Great Round—letting all of life into our consciousness. This is love. Put body to earth. Put soul to breath. Put mind in the great lap of Love. You are whole. You are utterly lovable. Permission granted. Take a moment, dear one. Root your feet on the earth, and read the words again. How does your body respond to this? Honor what comes forward, in the way that feels right for you. Holistic medicine and holistic living are not about substituting pharmaceuticals with herbs or achieving an ego-idealized self. They are about occupying a more feminine range with flexibility, responsiveness and accountability to the whole-that-we-are.

7.

Prayer of Sacred Release + Remember

To empty myself of old habits and unworkable patterns, I enter this prayer.
To make a gesture of self-cleansing, self-healing and self-awareness, I enter this prayer.
I seek to be fresh, to know the innocence of my heart, to be clear of diminishing thought and patterns of self-degradation that would pull me into self-pity and contraction.
Free of obstruction, I am renewed. Claiming my purpose, I am ready. Irrigating the seeds of my spirit, I am resourced. Knowing the radiance of my soul, I have a clear eye on my life.
My spirit, soul, mind and body vibrate the rhythms of power and peace as the cleansing waters wash through me. Free of trigger-ready reactions, I stand with my community. I sing the songs of my ancestors. In all I see, beauty and honor.
Becoming the seed, giving nourishment and receiving nourishment, I enter this prayer.

8.

As consciousness grows
We feel more
Not less
We can feel more pain
We can feel more grief
We can feel more sadness
Consciousness is not eliminating
It is adding, allowing
Consciousness is feeling everything
Turning from nothing
Not to endure,
But to feel all these feelings
As colors of the rainbow
Of love
What kind of rainbow
would we have
If there was only one color?

9.

Today is a day to be audaciously, lovingly, powerfully the magic that you are.

Dust off every criticism with compassion. We don't have to hold what people don't know against them.

Forgive and bless as you continue to be decisive, passionate and persistent in your service.

Remember the tricky curve of exponential change: when you look behind you, it looks pretty flat. When you look ahead, it appears as a wall.

Don't be fooled.

Rise.

10.

Deep Power
Isn't interested in safety
Its purpose is meant to frighten us
Out
Of stagnation
Pull us apart into
Deeper chambers of love
Dangle us
Above destinies that shine
I never said yes
To being a mother
Because I had the time
The expertise
The resources
The know-how
I said yes
Because the desire
To bring forth life
From within
Was my only reason for being
I never said yes
To my teachers
To deep committed learning
Because I had the money
Or the space in my schedule
I said yes
Because
I am crazy enough
To know
That my love
Creates everything

I need and desire
And so it is
I never said yes
To working with you
Because you are famous
Or because of your office
I said yes
Because long ago
Many years ago
You showed me the beauty
And ferocity
Of your heart
I've never forgotten
How could I forget
A heart like that?
Your deepest heart
Sings your deepest dream
Your dream for the people
Your dream for your life
When THAT dream
Takes precedence in your life
Mountains move
Divisions crumble
Schedules align perfectly
You become
A spiritual athlete
No avoidance
Only opening
To the moment
From your deepest
Heart
This is why I say yes

11.

Love is the only law I live by.
Conflict becomes Compassion
Control becomes Collaboration
Perpetrator becomes Protector
Victim becomes Vulnerable
Ambivalent becomes Accountable
Trauma becomes Initiation
Rescue becomes Refuge
Fissure becomes Communion
Anxiety becomes Fearlessness
Depressed becomes Resourced
You are not flawed and in need of fixing.
You are wild + holy and able to thrive.
You can do this.

12.

In each moment you are either committing fully to life or you are indulging a half-life.
It is that half-life that must be shed
Fully and completely
Compassionately removing its curse
Unapologetic for the ripples that may ensue
Sometimes it's not so much about mending your sorrows
As it is ending the practice of a living that creates them and the turning away from them as if they weren't your own flesh and blood.
Your journey of creation is a long one
And thank God for that
So much time and space to learn
Precisely
Intimately
The trustworthiness
Of living inside
Your own skin

13.

Past and future are created now, right where you stand.
Never separate from you.
There's no waiting to see what happens.
There is only a willingness to see that you are happening.
For so long it felt like my insides wanted out
But I couldn't trust
That what was inside me
Had a place in the outside world.
Deep trust is the outcome of deep participation.
The only one you need to trust is you.
And the only way to know what parts of you
Are trustworthy is to play with them.
Participate.
Choose.
Make beautiful messes that make bigger space for joy and sorrow.
It's not that you CAN create your life,
It's that you already do anyway, dear heart.
Let's create on purpose.

14.

A fire ritual
Under the waning moon
Emptying out
Freeing my soul's container
Liberating my mind spaces
Letting go of the grasp
I honor what is past
What must give way

15.

Beautiful, breathing being
The universe invites your exhale
Exhale your self-doubt into the infinite
Exhale the past you've been dragging around just in case
You need not justify your existence
Exhale
Exhale all you are complete with
All that is extra
Feel your breath free of imprint
Weightless
The lightest expression of spirit
Able to untether the heaviest particles
From your majesty
Able to deliver
You to
You
Exhale and be received into
The arms of love.

16.

Let us walk together where the earth is narrow
I will have faith in you until you have faith in you.
Every night our dreams unfold in secret.
The language of our own soul
Calling us into pathways
That gather us beyond realms of diminishment
Avoidance and anxiety
Into what finds us whole

17.

I want a life that seduces me.
A life I don't have to heal from
I don't want a better self-care routine.
I want a constant flirtation, a constant orgasm.
I don't want to be more organized or calm.
I want to live in a way that sets the heart of the world on fire.
This life happens in ordinary moments. It doesn't come from thinking positive, it is the song of the silent mind where all thoughts come from and to where they all return.
It's not letting go of what limits you, it's letting go of the belief you could ever be limited.
A willingness to let go of everything, all the time, now.
A life of seduction doesn't come from self-discipline. It is born of a knowing that something different can happen than what happened before.
Ordinary moments are extraordinary moments. These moments of your life yearn for your presence. Be here now. Fall in love with every broken dish, every cereal box, every embarrassment, every scar, every feather.
Let life love you by your willingness to see it for what it is—the kiss behind the kiss, the smile behind the smile, the sun behind the sun.
Make love to life. Make a life of love.

18.

Enter the temple
The temple of this moment
Everything you need is here
The medicine songs being sung for you
Since the day you were born
The ancestors are waiting for you here
In the temple of this moment
You become a hollow bone
In the temple of this moment
Intimate touch with those
Landmarks of human life
That underlie
And often interfere with
Daily living

19.

Dear Great Spirit,
Open me
Stand me in my full height
Pull back all the stops
That I may sense within myself the dignity of my bearing and my being
Stretch my fingers wide, wide, wide
Let me find a space for me, in my life
Have my connection and belonging nourish a greater web of reach—one that builds bridges
Without binding
Let all the little parts of me
Ripen like seeds in the soil
Like buds sweeping with themselves
Like fruit softening into the juicy fullness of promise
Let the mature and wise parts of me
Mother what has wanted to be small and sticky
Oh sweet and spacious one,
Expand me
I've done the inner work
My inner sanctums clear and open
These voices of love that echo
In the chambers of my heart
Now yearn to be a voice that brings others home
To theirs
Find me having conversations
Show me who needs to hear from me today
Help me to reach beyond myself
Help me to find you, in each one that I meet

RITUAL TO BLESS DECISION

My invitation is to begin owning your life now, by choosing to enter this ritual with me. If you do not enter this prayer-space with me now, don't let it slip through the cracks of excuses. Don't say, "I'll do it later; I'm just too busy right now." Simply say "NO."

And if you move through this portal now, let it be because you said yes. Fully. Cleanly. Completely.

When you go through the QR code portal, you'll be taken to a guided ritual that will utilize the journal prompts below, similarly to how we played with them in the desire space.

JOURNAL PROMPTS FOR DECISION

What is the purpose of this decision?
Who is this decision for?
Who is this decision *not* for?
What is there to gain by making this decision?
What must I be connected to in order to choose?
What do I fear I'll lose by choosing?
What am I trying to protect by delaying?
What shifts within me when I recognize my answer is only found right here, right now?
Where I have I projected the power of my decision onto another?
How do I practice reclaiming that power now?
How can I live my deepest values through my choosing?

CHAPTER 3

Surrender: Unguard Your Destiny

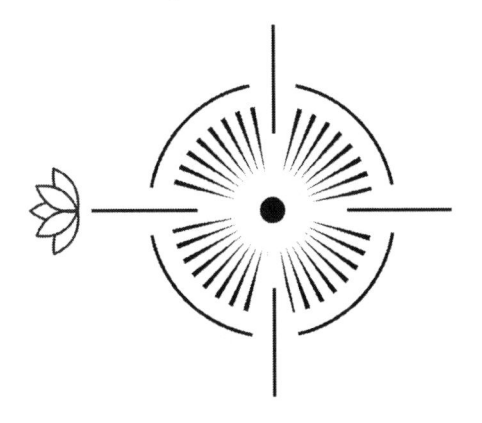

Set me free.
Let me fall,
So I remember
that I was made
To fly.

You are more powerful than you know. But your power doesn't come through muscling your way through your moments alone. In fact, the pushing, forcing and hyper-self-reliance crack and drain the deepest wells of your true potency. You are not alone. And you cannot struggle enough to find ease.

Surrender is what avails us to the limitless power of all creation. It is only in loving partnership with that-which-is-worthy-to-surrender-to that any real transformation or manifestation can be found.

We must be willing to become something unknown to our current selves. This is the adventure and the gamble. Our desires are inevitable. That much is certain. But what shape our selves will take to vibrate in alignment with that desire is something we can never know until we live into it.

Just as willingness to dissolve into surrender can give new meaning, form and energy to our lives, the shape of your suffering is moulded from your refusal to surrender. In shamanic perspective, decision does indeed create your life. But decision without surrender creates a life of control, manipulation and endless grasping.

Surrender is required because so much of our experience emerges from a space beyond conscious awareness. You don't see it coming. The moment you'll die and the way it will happen, the joke your son will tell that charms you, how your greatest dream will move from inspired idea into physical reality are all happening in a vast nexus of conditioned responses, cosmic forces, earth cycles and cultural programs. Your clearest decisions and deepest commitments hold potential to lead you on a path of rapture or a path of anguish. Your willingness to surrender is what determines both the quality and the outcome of your journey.

Without surrender, you are trapped by time. You'll race against it, feel it as a suffocating film constantly pressing in on you, a thief robbing you of freedom and joy. You will believe it to limit your creative potential, your effectiveness and even how much love you can give.

Surrender is what allows the inevitability of time to have meaning. Closely related to grief, surrender ends the feeling of being victimized, trapped or controlled by time. Grief is not sadness or simple loss, it is an alchemical process that shifts us from one identity to another. Surrender is the *yes* we say to this process.

When you lose a loved one, the self that you were with that person is no longer available. All the energy bound in that identity now runs free. Grief is the agonizing, ecstatic, even psychedelic process of the energy finding a new expression in you. It is our indwelling mechanism of transmutation, and whether it arrives as a brief moment of rapture upon recognizing that our world will never be the same, or as months of ache and hurt as we slough off the oldskin of a relationship, grief is a necessary part of any manifestation. The door to meaningful grief is surrender.

Time is not numbers on a clock. Time is change. The change from one thing to another is, in fact, the only way we can measure time or experience its existence. And what is change, other than energy being released from one form and finding another?

You cannot manage your way to time freedom. Becoming liberated and abundant inside of time requires you to meet thresholds of change with presence and the clear vision of your decision partnered with total surrender.

This moment, right now, is the opportunity. Move more breath into your body. Fill yourself with it. Be a breath glutton. Now hold your breath in, but don't become hard. Soften. Let your entire skin capsule unwind, as if you had sandbags on your shoulders, your hands, your legs. Now let that breath find its way out of you and into something else. Maybe a nearby insect breathes it in now. Or perhaps those molecules will choose to become part of a far-distant star. You are life, breathing itself into one form and then out again. When you recognize yourself as part of an endless, living continuum, you locate your natural capacity to release into its greater folds. No longer a single, solitary, tense thread, you feel the freedom of being the whole. Time is not separate from you. It is an expression of you, and you are an expression of it.

When familiar constriction, pressure, stress and tightening rise, conventional wisdom suggests that you learn to become more trusting of life. That you accept those around you as well as yourself. As well-meaning as this advice is, it doesn't go deep enough.

There is a difference between accepting that a person or circumstance is the way it is and having the capacity to truly let it in. The relaxing of our internal clench is only found in the latter.

You can track the difference between the two in the degree to which you consciously feel the impact of that person's way without fleeing, deflecting, identifying with or appeasing. When you are in the room with someone who holds a vastly divergent opinion from you on an issue you consider deeply important, you *can* successfully numb yourself through ignoring, defending, dissociating or playing nice. To truly accept and honor that the other has a right to their own life, mind and attitude can create a potential opening within you. But it's only when you keep opening—when you let the dissonance rise as heat from your belly to flush your face, hearing the blood throb in your ears as your breath becomes rapid—that something impactful happens.

Deep trust is not just accepting that the other person has a right to their life. It is letting the discord touch you, even jar you while you open to it. It is the ability to turn towards the wild and chaotic spirals of your actual life. Trust is the end of self-abandoning. It is meticulously sensing the fear that chaos will annihilate you and moving forward anyway.

Codependency is often misread as trust. When you barter your trust in exchange for the assurance that life will remain predictable, reliable, orderly and unchanging, you are only enacting codependent patterns. The quality of openness that you yearn for is only found in the most radical roots of trust. Real trust is a practice of continual opening, knowing that nothing stays the same. Real trust is an act of surrender.

Trust based on consistency will always leave you disappointed. Trust based on connecting to the ever-changing flow of life opens you to the deep magic always present in the world. Surrender is more than simple acceptance—as powerful as acceptance is. Surrender is the endless yoga of softening, suppling without ceding your center.

In preparing to write this missive, I had a dream. In the first scene, I was receiving an audio text from a client while around others in my home. Wishing to honor her voice and the privacy of our coaching space, I felt the need to sequester myself and to hold her message private rather than air it in front of others. I moved to the bedroom and closed the door. The moment I listened to the message in private, the scene shifted to a healing temple where women were anointing and blessing each other. It was an intimate space—small, but not confining. It was silent in that way that the most sacred spaces are, where you sense any words uttered become an unbreakable spell.

I looked over to the corner to find my client seated easefully in a full lotus posture while swallowing a sword. Her head rested back and the sword plunged so deeply down her throat that the hilt rested at her lips. It was clear that she had mastered this art. She was in unwavering ecstasy.

Sword swallowing as a physical discipline requires an incredible amount of presence and relaxation. Because the typical sword you would swallow passes between your lungs and close to your heart as it descends into your stomach, tightening your tissues or contracting can be deadly.

This dream gives us an image of surrender. It's our ability to master the art of encountering and taking in something that in many cases could be deadly and devastating. But due to our willingness to fully be here and to fully soften, we are not only unharmed but able to do the impossible.

The sword in this vision is decision. Decision is what gives meaning to the yielding. Without surrender, decision is ruthless. Without decision, surrender is self-indulgent, victimized and meaningless.

Powerful, successful women often believe that the ease they ache for is some sort of weakness, and they fear that it would mean the loss of all they've worked so diligently to create. And yet, there comes a threshold moment in every leader-woman's life where she will either metaphorically swallow the sword or slit her own throat—energetically severing her head from her heart and muting the flow of her life force.

This is why a woman can build an incredible team, have loads of support in her home and with her partner, and it never feels like enough. It never feels like she's fully off the hook; she can never walk out the door without her phone. She's going to be present either for the people in her life or for herself. Even as essential and incredible as it is for a woman to build a network of external support, if she hasn't the ability to surrender, she will walk alone.

Continuing to play out our lives inside this win/lose paradigm is not something we can afford—personally or collectively. It degrades the natural intelligence of life. Our cells no longer know what to do and become tumorous. We no longer see our own reflection in the petal of a flower. We become numb to the spectrum of aliveness unfolding within our own heart, our own breath.

Surrender is the alchemical process that reveals the truth: that when I win, you also win, and that in order for the collective to win, your win is essential. It ushers us from the either/or binary into the both/and of union.

To walk in the world surrendered is to have all your senses tuned into the heaven-on-earth that is already here. It is the opposite of scarcity. When we are open to life through surrender, we live in the delight that everything we want and need is already here.

You are emerging from the trance of scarcity. And just as the butterfly dwells in the pause of soft wings that must harden before her first flight, this departure from the paradigm of scarcity often has a period where you want so badly to believe abundance is real, but your habitual shapes have created a diseased allegiance to the idea that there is not enough.

And yet, a more ancient cosmic song persists in your cells. A memory rises of the truth that you were born into: that heaven-on-earth is here now. As a tiny child, you had the instinct that your environment gave you everything you needed. It was perfectly calibrated to you. Deep within your cellular memory, even if it's buried far in the unconscious, you possess a knowing that everything you need is here. Surrender is the portal that brings it from a fragment of memory that passes through you like a ghost to a way of living where desire is fulfilled automatically.

To live in surrender is to live a life of true audacity, because most of humanity is still living out the stale routines and habits of lack. Living in the frequency of surrender allows you to become truly generous, because you are tapped into the limitlessness of the Divine. The foundation of your life is no longer one of loneliness, struggle and anxiety. You are enfolded in the riches of this moment.

Surrender is the antidote to the codependency that cripples your superpowers. It allows you to place your clear decisions into God's hands and finally delivers others into God's hands as well. No matter how you identify that-which-is-bigger-than-you, surrender is always *to* those greater forces. Whether you name it Spirit, Nature, Coyote, Allah, Goddess or just the unnamable force that makes your heart beat and digests your food for you, it becomes your genuine creative ally inside of surrender. There is a sweet freedom in surrender-to that tastes unlike anything else.

Perhaps the most surprising thing about surrender is the degree of play that it awakens. When God is your creative partner, how could life be anything other than a creative playground?

Your persona will resist at times. It will continue to whisper or shout that only by being stressed, concerned, worried or, at minimum, serious, can anyone be certain that you care.

In the end, all surrender is surrender of persona. It is, I believe, what we humans are here to do. We are here living just as serpent does. Just as she sheds her skin, all in one piece, again and again, we shed the oldskin of persona. We let the waters carry the flow of life, needing neither to cling nor to push away. We live only to hold and be held by the joyous delight of desire and creation itself.

POEMS OF SURRENDER

1.

The mystic knows no separation
I am not what I am
I am what I am not
I become what I hate
I lose what I love
Until I love it all
Then
I
Am
Free
Free to be all and nothing
I die into life
Surrender into power

2.

Courting the Threshold

I am a creature of thresholds. As deep as I dance into the regular day and into the mystery of the other-world, it's that dance between—the stepping, the crawling, the giving and receiving of the threshold—that sets the rhythm in my blood and bones.

I greet the night by playing dead, turning my clothes backward and my mind inside out. I call everything far-flung back home to my heart and let it all drain to the earth.
I give back to the earth what is hers.
I give back what is hers.
I sweep thoughts like leaves out of my heart and give up this thing I call me.
I make space for the medicine that only arrives in Dreamtime.

The mornings belong to me. I wake up with no self most days, at least for a few moments. Sometimes Jaguar is pressed up behind me, her great form curled around my back, her purr thick like distant thunder.

3.

The fire of my love
Is an open secret

Come, sit beside me
I'll watch your eyes flash
Admire your toothsome smile
As we sing the old songs

There's a key
A code
You'll only know
Once you've entered

This is not for the rest of them
This is for the ones
Who dare and dream
In the dark
Many say they want to
Few actually do

4.

Blow my mind prayer

Dear Great Spirit,
Blow my mind today.
Smash my mental architecture like a toddler knocks over a block tower—joyfully, innocently and with delighted laughter.
Help me to dance in the chaos with a twinkle in my eye, knowing it is not punishment nor dark omen but only the supernova of the birth of my true self.
Let me fall a thousand times, so I can feel the unfailing generosity of the earth's embrace.
Let me stretch and activate to get up again.
Be Kali's sword.
Be Ereshkigal's eye.
Overwhelm me with such a flood of grace that the outcroppings of my denial and resistance cave and give way.
Knowing that my question is already answered, understanding that my desires are already actualized, show me how to dance more wildly inside of everything I used to name as negative, distracting or frightening.
Dear Sweet One, blow my mental constructs to smithereens so that I can flow back to my heart and womb once more.
Find me crumbling back home to my Self, and to you.
Show me how this is no act of violence, but a mercy. Give me eyes to see that these structures gave no safety but in fact were a cage of my own design.

Set me free.
Let me fall,
So I remember
that I was made
To fly.

5.

There are many ways to work with dreams and make purpose of their symbolic soul language. If you and I were sitting in a medicine circle together and you brought a dream, we might place our hands in each other's hearts, breathe together and become curious together about the dream, a missive happening through one woman's body but belonging to the whole.

Since we are connecting through cosmic rabbit holes, I'll invite you to answer, for yourself, the questions that come forward for me from this night of visions.

When was a time when you felt an emotion so powerful it had you shaking?

How did you meet that energy? Were you able to mobilize it?

What was trying to happen in that moment?

What is trying to happen, right now?

Have you ever gone to the earth as a guide or a support? If so, recall that experience now, including every sense that you can. Remember the smells, the sounds, the warmth or cold. Remember the time of day.

If you could ask the earth for a support right now, what would it be?

What is the transformation you might be avoiding that holds the key to your freedom?

6.

La Madrugada

When the plant people thirst
I answer
Making rain
Filling earthen cracks with prayers
And moisture
The Crow Clan
Gathers
Unapologetic loudmouths
Excited and eager
To pour their medicine into
My parched ears
Like water
Touching sacred ground
From nowhere
Hawk arrives
Letting himself be seen
Emissary of the heart
Be visible
I see you now
Radiant silence
Witnessing
The strength of song
Voice and heart
Come together as one
The silent praise of heart
Rising, soaring
To meet the dance of the throat

Today
Let every word I utter
Be jeweled with honoring
Let our laughter be gems dripping from our mouths
Let us create with joyful noise
And murmur prayers of remembering
The beauty of these gifts
Given so freely
Now all is quiet
No crow calls
Or whispers of hawk's skillful wing
Only the invitation
To live as this medicine
To let it be seen and heard
Through me

7.

You did not arrive to this world fearing the dark.

Your first nine months, growing, learning, listening, heart beating, there in the watery dark.

Yet the stories came early—how you were told to fear. Well-intentioned adults around you warning you to not wander off, to come in before dark. There are wolves out there. You might lose something out there. Monsters hide their fearsome shapes out there. What they don't tell you is that there's something that's been lost in the plain light of day. That the light can't protect you from what the over-culture has taken. Far more monsters roam in the light of what we know than what we know not.

The more we turn from what is dark, the more we lose our ability to see into deep and quiet spaces.

It's blindness that's hurting us, unwillingness to see, not dark.

8.

When the mind won't slow,
Don't fight it
Go to the heart instead.
Feel how much you love
How much you love
The one you love
Not generalities,
Specificities
Holding her hand
Seeing her smile
Feel your love for your children
A uniqueness of each of them
Feel it in your body
Feel how much you love
Making a difference in this world
Something so small
That actually changes everything
Think of the one person
Who will sleep easier
Because of who you choose
To be
Don't fight with the thoughts
Don't push down the restlessness
Just turn towards the quiet rest
Of what really matters

9.

An unobscured sky, magnificent blue
Held TWO eagles in my view
Both were being chased by smaller birds, just playing their role in the order of things.
I take the medicine to be: partner with others who seek to soar, who hunt with a broad view.
Let the others peck. It's just their way.

10.

In my journey this morning, Owl retrieved a message.
The path is completely certain.
The path is absolutely unknown.
This message is a reminder. It's not new. It reminds us that we can rest into this moment, knowing that everything we seek to accomplish is already done. It is certain.
At the same time, miracles live only in the unknown. We have to open to everything unknown to create the path forward.
The unknown is not an enemy, it is the sacred ally.
What can you delight in NOT knowing today?
Who is your ally?
What happens in your body if you relax into knowing that everything, everything is being taken care of?

11.

You find me in the dreamlands
Hands extended out
Reaching
You transcend space and time
For the sake of connection
I need you to know
I'm listening
I need you to know
I'm here
Our crazy minds think
Getting to the goal
Will be confident strides
In wide open spaces
But it is this
Being in a cave
So dark you can't see
Taking one step
Then another
Slow
Feeling your way
Reaching your hands
Into the thick dark
Know that I'm the dark
I'm here
I'm stepping with you
What you seek
Seeks you also
The peace you seek
Seeks you also

The sanity you seek
Seeks you also
The expansion you seek
Seeks you also
The love you seek to express
Seeks to be expressed through you
Also
You don't walk alone
Sweet friend
A deeper magic in you
And all around you
Powerful one
Only those who succeed, fail
Only by failing can we succeed
Surrender
Surrender
Surrender
All is coming
All is here
Now

12.

The bliss of grief
Something moves through me
That is not my
own
Seeks me
Thrums its rhythm in my
throat and my
ear
It gathers itself
In my
Eyes
Blurry until clear
Seeing now, steady now
Rolling down my
Cheeks
Place a tear on the
Earth
For the ancestors
Drum your rhythm
For their memory
For you
Are their dream come
True

13.

The opposite of peace is not chaos
The opposite of peace is unwillingness
I am unwilling because I hurt
I hurt because I love
The less I love, the less I feel
The less I feel, the less willing I am
The more I love, the more I feel
The more I feel, the more I *can* feel
The more I can feel, the more I can love
The more I can love, the more peace I have

14.

Water Elemental

Let us honor sacred flow today
Let us feel your cool, fluid power
I pause at river's edge
To see you reflect my beauty
And to see your beauty
Reflected in me

15.

Suddenly, grief
A movement in the trees
The wind lovingly sculpting the leaves
A lover's kiss
It all comes out
My people's pain
All of them.

Not just clients
Not just family
Not just people
Who live nearby
Not just ones who look
And talk like me
But all
Who have
Forgotten

Forgetting who we are
The language of our hearts dims
Our minds absent from our mouths
Vulnerable to false stories

Forgetting
Just getting through the day to
Collapse
We cease to respond creatively
To pain

I cry for our forgetting
And for our remembering
You and me
Re-member
Re-source
Re-cover
A grief song
Winds over
Rivers of tears
May all beings remember to hear
The voices in their hearts

16.

Give the earth your tears
When you cry, when you weep
When flow of emotion becomes
River in your body
Too strong to push down

Give the earth your tears
When salt carves a path
Down the sweet lines
Of your face
Let it fall
Into her softness, her stone
Wipe your eyes
With your hands
The wings of your heart
And from your wings to her body
A wet blessing

The earth feels everything
You have ever felt
She feels all the things
You couldn't feel
She is mother aching
To comfort
Her weeping child

This is a way of honoring
Of giving back
This is a way
Of love becoming love

17.

If you cry today
Give your tears to the earth
Carry the tiny ocean
On fingertip and plant it
As a seed
Of the wonder
Of being alive
Of feeling this deeply
Give your tears to the earth
Mark the holy ground where you stand
Sanctify this opening
This release
This wetness
This blessing

18.

The star and the snake
Live inside my womb
Constellating
Contemplating
Conspiring
To birth anew
A new mind
A new vision
A new way
Will you join me?

19.

Wet, cold, yin
Red-winged blackbirds click
In curiosity
Forty degrees
Wind and rain
Springtime gifts

RITUAL OF SURRENDER

Now I ask you to trust me more than you trust yourself. Lean into the fabric of it. Feel the rough and smooth of taking what you've done unconsciously and accidentally for so long and now making it intentional.

In the ritual you'll access through the QR code, I invite you into a ritual of not-knowing. We rely on what we think we know, and thus our knowing is fecund ground for practicing surrender. Work with the journal prompts below to deepen.

JOURNAL PROMPTS FOR SURRENDER

What are my current criteria for trust? Do they require an update?

Where do I feel most intimate and at ease with surrender?

What conditions facilitate my willingness to release and be supported?

What if we can all win?

What have I learned and developed that I can now entrust to another?

What feels extra in my life right now?

Where am I holding too tightly?

What am I worrying about that is not actually mine to hold?

When was a moment of total surrender that felt amazing?

What questions do I need answered in order to surrender more fully?

Who stands to gain something from my surrender?

Who stands to lose something from my surrender?

How can I love myself more through deeper surrender?

CHAPTER 4

Inspired Action: Demonstrate Your Destiny

You are the rain on parched earth
You are the song of the raindrops
You are the language of thunder
That reverberates through the heart
You are flashing tongues of lightning
Licking the ground
Like a ravenous goddess

> You are the inspiration
> That calls the rainbow
> Into form
> You are the petrichor

Inspired action is love-in-motion. In it you are animated by the codes you came here to live—boundlessness, mercy, possibility. You are the clear, uninterrupted silence of your being, come to life.

Inspired action is the child of genuine excitement. It is a previously invisible horizon coming into view. Suddenly there is more to life than you realized, and you feel the irresistible pull to move. You've had those moments, when color became more vivid, life became more precious, smells became more acute and you felt all parts of you unified in shared purpose. Like the first days of falling in love, when you seem to need no sleep, hours of conversation flow like minutes and the whole world seems to rearrange itself to your purpose. You are baptized with clarity, and what previously appeared as an imposing limit now looks like an invitation.

Limits are not wrong or bad, and they need not be fearsome. They have no bearing on whether or not you can manifest the life you desire. They provide a meaningful opportunity to cleanse your relating with this moment now, to ensure you don't go too far from yourself. But to believe that you must justify your desires or the actions they require by overcoming limits is to build your life on ground that cannot hold you.

The lie is that someday, once you've overcome all the limits and obstacles, you'll finally cross the finish line. You'll make the sale, give yourself permission, believe in yourself, close the deal, get the award—and then somehow live happily ever after. You'll stop pushing so hard. You'll open up, soften your gaze. But in reality, overcoming obstacles is nothing more than a paradigm rooted in a belief that if you clear one more mindset block, you'll be free. The problem with this is that overcoming one obstacle just leads to the next obstacle. The obstacles never end. Obstacles become the primary relationship in your life.

Freedom is not found by overcoming limits. It is living without them.

The path of limitlessness is the path of inspired action. Transcending limits is not where freedom is born. Freedom emerges from claiming and being claimed. In the moments you've felt most free in your body, it wasn't because you overcame something. It wasn't giving yourself permission. It was rooted in a moment of revelation and mutual possession. Being pregnant for the first time, for example, causes a woman to face a complex reality. For nine months and beyond she will not get smaller, as our current cultural ideal suggests she ought to. And at the same time, her physical expansion is literal evidence that she is, indeed, the source of life itself. Claiming both sides of her reality and letting her body transcend her opinion of it will open her to a greater dimension of intimacy, joy, disgust and fascination with her form. She will move into unbounded aliveness. That aliveness will be evident in her words, her tears, the degree of availability she has for others, what she eats and when. It will evidence itself through her labor and delivery as well as in her relationship with her child. It is communicated through her actions into the world, not just as she brings her child into the world but for the rest of her life. Her expression of the Mother archetype will flow joy rather than duty as its primary frequency.

There is a claiming and being claimed that is carried through inspired action. And in that embrace, true ground gathers within you and beneath you. Your life begins to feel like your own and at the same time a mystery that holds you firmly without ever fully revealing its face.

There is something in you that wants life to yield to your yearning. That wants to deeply and viscerally experience the difference your life makes in the world. You also crave to hear the language of life and to answer it. You don't just want to leave your mark. You want to become so merged and fluid in your life that you can pull honey from stone.

How you know that you've decided and surrendered is that you feel inspired to act. The action may or may not seem like it has a linear path to your desired outcome. You may even doubt it will work. It might arrive oddly, your mind unlocked so suddenly and completely that your body shudders with recognition. Inspired action never arrives as a plan, a chain of events or a series of clear instructions. It is only the internal lightbulb that goes on. You see an action that can meaningfully move you towards the goal, and you take it. No waiting. No consideration or weighing pros and cons.

These actions, born of a shift in consciousness, feel light and clean in our bodies. They leave no residue. And though we can doevolve into resistance, these actions arrive as something we know we must do. They are rooted in a body-level knowing.

Inspired action is as light as feathers and as impactful as death. For any of us who are mothers, you hold in your mind the memory of your child bringing you a gritty fistful of dandelions. This action that endeared to you a creature you thought you couldn't love more wasn't potent because it was premeditated or even unique. It was because the act was born of love and honest care. And those dandelions, which doubtless closed even before the day was done, awakened something in you that matters.

The women I support are all high achievers. They feel the tug of a mission in their bones, and their instinct is to respond. They are no strangers to completion, to actualization, to turning their ceilings into floors. These are people of great heart, and yet all the compulsory doing can numb them to the genuine excitement and passion they had for their craft in the first place. The shift to inspired action from calculated action is what moves them from the dull, mundane world of routine and into the non-ordinary state of bliss that is their birthright.

This shift is uncomfortable. Just as Stockholm Syndrome can develop between a person and their abuser, coping mechanisms of self-harm can develop from chronic pushing and force-based action. We come to trust the feeling of exhaustion more than that of freedom. Inspired action is never forced. It arises from within. You have a deep *want* to do it. To do only what you want to do is a radical act for a woman. To listen deeply, past your programming, is to access the hidden reservoirs of freedom and magic that most people will never experience.

Imagine a life where you have the sensitivity to recognize and honor your needs for movement, play, sweat, sex and screaming. Imagine what it would be like to both feel when you need to set your work down and also act on that impulse. Imagine an unshakable knowing that the life you love comes from taking actions you love and refusing to take any actions you don't. This is the promise of inspired action.

Inspired action is genuine embodiment. Embodiment is not just knowing you are powerful or even feeling powerful. It's when your actions demonstrate your power to the degree that others recognize it. You know you are embodying your vision when your environment reflects it back to you. While it's absolutely true that manifesting an incredible life is 90% internal work, internal work is not enough. The degree to which we are not speaking our truth, acting out our truth, taking risks on behalf of our truth is the degree to which we are still allowing someone else to run our lives.

The red roots of our ancestral lines have been polluted for untold generations with the disease of looking for an outer authority. Lacking any recognizable puberty rites, most of us never shift from pulling our projections of God off of mother and father, and for our whole lives we continue to look to some person, some system, some outer authority to show us what is right and good. This is why the desires that arrive to powerful women—which often seem vague or fanciful to them at first, such as buying land and building a retreat center—are so important to define through inspired action. These are often the beginnings of a wise impulse to create new initiations and ceremonies that can usher us forward both personally and collectively.

You may have gone through your whole life without receiving meaningful instruction on how to feel what genuinely excites you and to follow the feeling. Instead you were conditioned into compulsory action. Thus the distinctions between a worthy action that might stretch your current skill set and an action taken to avoid a perceived cause of suffering or to please an authority figure were not made.

The way you can recognize the difference between a worthy-but-stretchy action and a compulsory action is the presence of lack. Inspired action *will* call you to stretch. But it happens from a deep sense of fullness, of bounty. The fabricated reality of lack you dwell inside of takes your inborn and natural care for the other and twists it into either competition or pity. Your inborn capacities for leadership and collaboration are squelched when you compete for resources you perceive as limited. Your destiny of fully unfurling, enjoying and fostering overabundance becomes alien to you, as you worry that your having is taking from others.

When acting by force, living inside the shrunken and fearsome confines of scarcity, your life will never make sense. You can't make others wrong enough to feel right, even if you are wronging capitalism or patriarchy. Everything you want is already here. You don't need to overcome a limit or annihilate a competing value system in order to access it. The greatest waste of life isn't trying for something that was never possible; it's sitting in the middle of paradise and missing it entirely.

We could name inspired action as creativity. But I choose to not use that word as it is so often associated with having to make something up. Our conversation here is about the ripening of seeds already dwelling within. As those seeds take root, there is a natural, effortless impulse that arises from within you. This action is not only joyful and effortless. It carries the frequency of your desire fulfilled. It will terrify your persona and move the warm glow of your inner knowing out into the world.

The poems held within this text are a hundred-plus expressions of inspired action. At no point did I have a cerebral thought that I wanted to publish a book and that I ought to start writing poetry from my dreams. The words simply began to arrive. They illuminated my body. I felt fully online, fully awake. And as these words continued to come, I knew I needed to capture them. They come and then they go. So it is with inspired action. It must be taken the moment it arrives.

Because inspired action breaks you from the habituated self, your persona will do nothing but complain. I promise you, the more you thank the persona for its contribution and send it off while you embody the life force flowing through you, the more your life will truly be the heaven on earth it was meant to be.

Gradually you will allow yourself the grief of recognition that others will not choose to live this way. You will remember that you can love them anyway. You will remember that you can love you anyway. You will move like thunder across the land of your life, and you will also become the thirsty soil sated by the rains the storm brings.

Day by day, you will practice manifesting a life you love—and not just by sitting on a cushion and visualizing it or by creating a plan that is really just a control mechanism. You will feel the whisper in your ear to dance your dance of crazy wisdom. You will follow it. You will become an undulating spiral of creativity, possibility and genuine participation in the song of life in the unique way for which you are made.

POEMS OF INSPIRED ACTION

1.

Your voice is powerful.
Give it to praise today in whisper or laughter.
Let your voice and your choice shake the earth today with the joy that is your being.
Create the coming time of dark as what you declare it to be, not what you fear it could be.
Be bold, my friends.

2.

I dreamed this for you

I am in my home, alone. It is darkest night. I am alone and afraid. All around the house, men are gathered. Each holds a candle. They don't speak or move but stand, soft and firm, their numbers extending as far as I can see.
They are all ages, all races. Still. Searching me.
I cower towards the ground, crawling on my belly, hoping they don't see me. I am terrified of them and my body shakes with the fear.
Yet.
Beneath fear is a knowing. I know these men have assembled around in me peace. They mean no harm. As the shaking reaches my core, it doesn't land there. It doesn't match.
Instead of crawling, I lay my belly flat to the earth. Surrendered to her, I feel for her counsel.
A knowing rises. I know what I must do. I must stand.
Suddenly I am outside. I stand on a pyre.
One by one the men come, lighting, growing the fire with their candles.
I burn but am not harmed. I am free.
One by one, the men pass through the fire with me. We are free.
This is not a fire of endings, but of beginnings.

3.

Ways

There is the right way and the wrong way.
And then there's your way.
A wild way
A way of spirals and songs more than straight lines
A way that calls you from deep within
From the mouths of your ancestors
From depth of caves and crash of waves
The way you go when you live by the vision of the stars in your womb
And the sight of your deep eye

4.

The Wild in Me

A part of me wants to be in the circle, doing circle things. Sharing, circulating, listening, relating.

I am woman, but I am also coyote.

I pace.

The circle I make is the dancing blade-edge where firelight shimmers into darkness. From your seat close to the fire you peer out, seeing me laughing. It's easy to think I'm laughing at you, but I'm just laughing because life is so crazy and beautiful and wise.

I've always been a creature of edges, of places where two things meet, where they are learning if and how to be One.

Not long ago, I had a dream. In the dream I was swimming in the ocean with a man. In "real life" we had gone to grade school together. In the dream he was attractive and charming, making vulgar advances towards me. I rebuked him.

I took this dream into my Journey Meditation. I asked the Ocean, "What do you want me to know?"

She showed me how I am a tiny speck on the surface of soul, and what fathomless depths exist below my kicking feet. She wanted me to see that I was so much more expansive than I allowed myself to believe. She showed me how I believe the tiny speck has to "hold it all together" when in truth, there is an ocean of Being, buoying me up.

In my Journey, I also asked the man in my dream to reveal himself, truly. He peeled off his skin and became a sort of Pan

God. His eyes were bright but his skin was ruddy. I asked, "Why have you come? What do you want? What should I know?"

He told me, "I need to be free, to roam, to play, to explore. I have been waiting for so long. And I am so lonely for you."

He is the piece in me that pushes upward now, like a flower in bloom, like the *I Ching*. All my antennae are tuned to the vibration of release, and freedom. I've been living one story for so long, and the wild in me has sat somewhat patiently in the corner. Now it is the wild's turn. I release my identity, at least for now. At least for this moment. I find time and space away. The scent in the bloom of my heart speaks: my need for nonconforming life and unconventional living are far beyond what I think will be acceptable.

We always like the idea of the wild. We like it as a concept—distant, disembodied. Now the yip-yip-howl of Coyote calls it in. All the places in you that you can't quite inhabit, everything that won't behave, won't make sense, all your bad habits, all the ways you resist: this is your wild. This is the thing in you that won't be possessed or tamed. Stop trying to tame it! Stop trying to make it fit the shape of your ideals. Let it off its leash. Stand up and dance your Coyote dance at the wild edge where darkness romances light.

Arrive to your life in unapologetic celebration, checking your holistic intentions at the door. You won't need them where we're going.

If you are a wild Coyote, if you are tired of domestication, come find me. Let's dance this crazy, wild and wise path together.

5.

Will you take a moment
With me
Right now
This moment
To bow to what is most alive?
Be it a sigh of relief
The bite of heartburn
The way the sun moves
Against a wall just now
Perhaps it's death that's
Most alive now
Or a pesky virus whose
Lusty will to live
Has hijacked the will
Of your immunity
Or maybe the cadence
And rhythm of the voices
Around you
So plain and powerful
And dear.
Love this aliveness
With me.
Stop. Breathe it in.
Fill the bucket
So to empty it again.
It is you
It is you
It has always been you

6.

Making my offer to Mother River today, the raucous song of the ravens greets me.
The mists rising off of Her waters baptize me anew, kiss me on the forehead and bless my grateful smile.
You have a deep connection with nature and the animals. Let them pull you into natural time today.
Pause, to listen to Raven.
Pause, to let the sun kiss your cheek.
Pause, to open your arms to the wisdom of an oak.
Pause until you can feel that love seeping into your bones like mist into air.

7.

Dear Great One,
Help her to remember to love this day.
Help her to remember Who She Really Is.
Help her to remember the joy of having a voice that carries far.
Help her in all the ways she is wanting help.
Help her to remember that she carries all hearts in her own, and that all hearts carry her too.
Help her to remember that she is never alone.
Help her to feel the line of her ancestors in her back, supporting and stabilizing her in their ancient ways.
Help her to feel the Spirits who are so devoted to her, that wait at the tops of trees and inside acts of brave mercy.
Help her to smile and let her body shake with laughter.
Help her to remember that the ones who are so contracted and angry are really just afraid, and that they still worry that there are snakes at the bottom of the bed.
Help her to remember that time does not heal all wounds, but that it is in honoring and acknowledging the wound consciously that all healing is found.
Remind her that she carries the love of the ancients in her breath and gaze.
Help her to stand when others shrink.
Help her to love herself as her own father and mother loved her, and still do.

8.

Dear Mystery,
Be in my life today. Walk with me in my highest timelines.
Pervade my field. Bless every being with whom I cross paths.
Bless my speech, ride on my breath, inform my words.
Light my vision.
Be in every communication I send, every message, every post.
Bring your beauty, wisdom, majesty and magic through me and every action I take.
Invoke yourself through me.
Be in my dreams and my creations.
Be in my life today and let me be with you.

9.

The Earth wants to hold you in her mossy, ancient, loving arms. She wants to bathe you in golden beams and remind you that authentic grounding happens when you rest in her presence. Healing happens with ease when you let yourself sink into her rhythms.
Breathe.
How many times have you tried to outpace her by staying in your busy constructs?
How many times have you neglected her medicine by turning to numbing agents, your devices and vices?
How many times have you said, "I'll make time for you," only to stay holed up in the darkness?
And yet, she still holds space for you to return to her. She still saves a spot for you in the forest. She still gives you her medicine willingly.
Today (and every day) you have a choice: become the feral creatrix you were meant to be
Or keep holding yourself in stagnation.
My invitation to you is to step outside, even in the cold of winter, and embrace what's in front of you.
You, your business, your relationships . . . none of it flows until
your nature
your clarity and
your connection to the Earth are made.

10.

Your life is a perfect mirror
Of your inner being
If you don't like what you see outside
Look within
Love yourself so deeply
That it echoes through your reality
So much that it rings a bell
In every soul surrounding you
And don't love like love is an idea
A thought
Let love be your action
Create your day in love, with love,
Through love
The first 30 minutes of your day
Sets the tone for your life
Instead of newsreels, scrolling, worry and habit
Do something different
Breathe
Pray
Feel grateful
Notice beauty
Intend
Create
Make your day as you seek it to be
And so shall it be

11.

The trees are singing your name
Today
The grasses weep at the
Beauty of your
Heart
The stars heed the call
To illumine your wildest
Dreams
As the earth receives your
Untethered sorrow
Blessed be
Blessed be
Blessed be

12.

We are not happiest when things go the way we want them to. We are happiest when we are able to make meaning of the way things are happening.

13.

You are the rain on parched earth
You are the song of the raindrops
You are the language of thunder
That reverberates through the heart
You are flashing tongues of lightning
Licking the ground
Like a ravenous goddess
You are the inspiration
That calls the rainbow
Into form
You are the petrichor

14.

You are the Mystery, becoming naked to itself
Don't confuse the concept of certainty with the power of what you are.
Touch the sunyata.
This day, the day ahead of new moon is the day of the Void. It's the day when emptiness stretches its jaws wide and receives whatever is placed within. It's the ultimate place of all comings and goings, the great fruitful darkness from which everything emerges and to which everything returns. Moment by moment. You are not a result of the past. You are not what you believe yourself to be. The past is caused by the present, and the future is created right here and now.
The Void creates. Being creates.
Take this day to make relationship with the Mystery in you, before painting over it with intention.
Be purposeless. Let yourself be spooked and spooky by the power of what you really are.

15.

There's a new life growing inside me
Meaning into intention
Energy into form
Intelligence into coherence
It's not a child I'm preparing to birth
I'm creating a universe
A cosm to whisper itself into a chasm
Widening circles of connection
Where separation once held strong
Such lust for life that I became the vessel
For something yet unseen
Like the pregnant seeds snoring
Beneath sleeping layers of
Snow and ice
I can't see them
I know they're there
We breathe together now
Each inhale, a language I barely
Comprehend
Each exhale
A genuflect to a mystery
My thoughts can't hold
Now my mind broadcasts the signal
My heart a magnet for everything I
Ever held myself apart from

16.

I enter the eye
Of the Great Mother
I become nothing
One with everything
Inside of her blackness
Sound from other times
Like boxes turning over
Gallops
Bells
Eerie shrieks
Everything happens here
It all happens here

RITUAL OF INSPIRED ACTION

The beauty of ritual is that its power is rooted in love and gratitude. In the ritual you'll find through the QR portal, I'll share with you a delightfully easeful ritual to move you out of heaviness and duty and into moment after moment of inspiration and flow. You can partner with the prompts below to activate the frequency of inspired action within you.

JOURNAL PROMPTS FOR INSPIRED ACTION

What helps me to take inspired action?

Where do I already sense the medicines of emerging and thriving in my life?

What role has duty played for me recently?

Where am I using the energy of duty and compulsion?

What could my life look like if that changed?

What do I fear I'll lose if I make that change?

What happens in my body when I sense the possibility of living and acting from an inspired place within me?

What thoughts give me confidence to explore following my desire through action?

CHAPTER 5

Receiving: Have Your Destiny Now

You unfold conflict into intimacy
You show us what is shared
Beneath the wrongs we scold
I can't resist you

To receive is to become whole in the wheel of aliveness. To live the depth of receiving we are actually capable of is to live the beauty way. Beauty rests on blessing. Without blessing, no beauty can exist. To receive, rather than merely to possess or know, is to see the face of God everywhere you turn. It is the kiss behind the kiss, the touch behind the touch.

In receiving we are again changed. Our lives become a visible beacon of what was before invisible. It is the harvest, born of the faith invested in the seed of intention and in the participation of the Unknown.

So much of the confusion around manifestation and the feeling of being imprisoned within limits is sourced in an unripened ability to receive. One of the favorite phrases of our time is to "release that which no longer serves." Far too infrequently is the question ever asked which part of us believes we could *not* be served by life. It's only from the narrow crevice of the persona that anything, ever, could seem useless. Rather than reacting to the sting of discomfort with automated "release," you have the opportunity to become like a child once again. Feel the texture of moment with your fingers, take it into your mouth. Ask what this flavor might be trying to gift you.

When you open to the full territory of receiving, you burn open like a field on fire. You recognize that your ability to say yes or no to something rests only in your present-moment choice, informed by nothing other than your desire and decision. A contentious relationship, the experience of diminishment through someone's comments, even internal thoughts that seek to limit your scope can all serve you. You can receive something of value from them, and you can still send them away.

You have no obligation to say yes to an experience just because you feel like you're getting benefit from it. Continuing to hang on to clients who don't show up in sincerity to the work; a job that provides "security" but acts as a succubus; or even a way of eating that can get you to your health goals but feels lifeless—all these situations are opportunities to say no. Receiving is what allows you to come out of the trance of powerlessness and scarcity. When you live inside the practice of receiving from all of life, letting it touch you deeply, you simultaneously allow the Mystery to give light to your life.

At a root level, you come out of your inner authority and authenticity only because you seek to avoid pain or you are grasping for pleasure. The avoidance and grasping arise from a false idea that something you don't like is *only* painful and "negative" and something you idealize is *only* pleasurable and good. You might judge others, or even yourself, for not 'eating clean' because you've decided that there is one right kind of diet and to deviate from that can only lead to illness. Or you might have a relative that always seems to trigger the worst in you and you've decided that triggering is definitely bad and so seek to avoid the person. When I say "decide," please hold it lightly. Most of the decision is happening outside the scope of your conscious awareness. In moments such as these, you are living only half a life and you don't even know it.

When you choose instead to receive the fullness of your relative and your chosen diet, cascades of freedom are unleashed within you. In seeing that there is pain even in the pleasure of clean eating, you are able to choose your preferred way of eating, but you take no offense if others choose to eat differently or even if you deviate. Seeing that there is not only goodness in your relative but pleasure held within the experience of being triggered, you have no more need to conform and limit your life with avoidance. You are empowered to make an honest choice in the moment.

Receiving is what allows for meaning and meaninglessness. Inside of this freedom, we access a deeper, more authentic level of desire. There is no longer an invisible finger at your back, always poking you and pushing you forward. In truth, nothing has any meaning—we are the ones who create meaning. As the great sage Shankara said, "All of life is simply waves of beauty and bliss, neither inauspicious nor meaningful." To receive is to taste the truth that you can assign any meaning to what is happening or none at all. You become the storyteller rather than identifying with the story.

Receiving is actualization. It is result. It is love made real. There is something primal in you that longs for completion. And not just the surface-level satisfaction of checking off a to-do list; it wants to experience the reflection of your willingness to bring love, care and devotion through your actions.

The distortion of this inborn yearning for actualization is trying to prove or earn worth through constant output. Your busyness is like junk food for the parts of your architecture that are designed to be fueled with true purpose. Receiving dismantles the walls you erect through the numbing of activity. It puts you back in touch with the inherent gifts you bring to the community of life, simply by being who you are. The more you inhabit the frequency of receiving, the more you experience the truth that actually, nothing is ever earned. Everything is freely given.

Receiving places us back in the cradle of the Divine. It is truly the end of scarcity paradigm. Receiving leads to a level of honesty and authenticity that is inaccessible any other way. You can be married yet not actually receive the love of your partner. The moment you receive that love, hold it, taste it, let it all the way in, your trauma bonds come undone. The spell that you are unlovable and unworthy is broken. When you shift your focus from "doing the work" to rid yourself of shame or heal trauma and simply practice receiving the love that is being offered in each moment, you live your real life.

Receiving, like her sister aspects on the Wheel, is a way of being in the world. To live inside of it is to commit to dwelling within abundance every day, every moment, for the rest of your life.

It expresses itself as greater sensitivity to the world around you. The more you open, to fully receive and be touched by what you used to ignore, dismiss, cast off or resist, the more you are able to experience the subtle layers of all of life—the lineage of words, the ancestry of pain, the ultimate outcome, years down the line, becomes visible in patterns unfolding now.

It begins as simply as being present to sensation. When you brush your teeth tonight, let yourself actually feel the engagement of your arm, the expert and masterful articulation of your fingers around the brush. Let your ears be delighted by the scratchy and repetitive sh-sh-sh as the brush moves over your teeth and the explosion of sensation on your tongue as the bristle scrape this intelligent flesh. Come alive in your life where you have been sleeping. Any moment is a ripe opportunity to receive.

Your inborn abilities to create and experience meaning are amplified in receiving. You find yourself living in a world of limitless support, limitless connection, limitless possibility. I've witnessed countless women become more responsive to the clear inner directive for revolution, for cultural change, that their soul requires, through their willingness to receive more.

And I've witnessed these women encounter confusing ceilings—on the level of love in their romantic partnerships, on their money, on their health. Often mistaken for a sign that she's done something wrong or "it wasn't meant to be," these moments of pain and confusion are only feedback on the level of authenticity they've been living. A woman's natural state is to receive her inner and outer world fully and without restraint.

Every single time I've supported a woman in untethering herself, it has been through a discovery of how, though she appears to let herself be supported, she still harbors a deep unavailability to life. There is some part of her that she is withholding out of fear that if she goes all in, life will let her down. This leads to a rigidity easily mistaken for genuine resilience. But it's brittle rather than supple. Their bodies reflect this, as elevated shoulders and tight necks attempt to lift up a body that was supported by the earth all along.

To fully receive is an art form. To simply welcome the sensation when someone compliments your dress without needing to explain, tell a story about it or immediately deflect by returning the compliment is to unleash an incredible spectrum of sensation and power. Likewise to simply allow someone to apologize without appeasing is a level of intimacy that has the power to create a new world.

In full transparency, receiving is the aspect of the Wheel that remains most mysterious to me. I find growth edges in all aspects, but in this one the most. From my confusion, I understand that receiving itself can bring us closer to the heart of the Mystery without anything to do but open and allow and let life in, knowing that it will shape every moment going forward. The Mystery cannot be explained and any attempt to categorize or define is a disservice. I invite you to stop your seeking to understand what I'm suggesting. Simply notice what opens in you as you receive it.

The overlay our culture places on the magic of receiving is obligation. Words of praise spoken out of duty, gifts given without heart degrade our collective energy and pull us further from ourselves, and each other. In every single instance, these displays uphold the persona and shut out the real human being behind it. They are liminoid rather than liminal—they attempt to bring a new shape to life without actually being touched. The persona will always avoid intimacy, for it is in intimacy that the persona is undone and the real human being comes forward.

Throughout human history and culture, the most important moments of receiving were held in ceremony. To receive a new name, to receive adulthood, to receive the blessing of your ancestors—all of the people in our bloodlines recognized that receiving was a transformational act and required a container that could fully metabolize the energetic catharsis. Today we lack such structures and most receiving has been trivialized, commercialized and unrecognized.

The consequences of this are dire. Without proper containers for transformation, you go through initiation processes half-baked. You fail to fully live your life because you are terrified to do the very thing humans are made to do—to shed one identity completely and take on the new.

In the Bhagavad Gita, Krishna teaches Arjuna about the nature of existence. He instructs Krishna that just as one takes off one's soiled clothes at the end of the day for fresh new clothes, so too at the end of one's life, one takes off the soiled and worn identity in favor of a new one. What is grossly misunderstood is that Krishna was not just talking about physical death. You are made for your ego persona to constantly die and be reborn many times within the body you are in now—you are a phoenix. Without the ability to receive, to go through these necessary ego deaths and rebirths, unable to let life find a place within you, you will always walk through this world estranged and in a state of contraction.

We do have ways of institutionalized recognition and honoring of some of these thresholds of initiation, such as the quinceañera, baptism, graduation, funeral and wedding. They provide sanction for the institutions that created them. But the center of gravity of our personal and collective values are shifting. We do not necessarily want to give or receive sanction from these religious, cultural and political institutions. Our current institutions fail to recognize that initiation continues throughout our adulthood. We need rites of passage for divorce, miscarriage, breaking through glass ceilings, menopause, emptying the nest, the end and beginning of female friendships. When these very real moments of transmutation fail to be recognized, our mooring is lost even more. Rather than sanctioning governments or religious institutions, we need ceremony that sanctions Spirit, the Land and most importantly, the organizational structure of human connection and love.

By strengthening your skill and intimacy with receiving, you awaken and catalyze your inborn capacity to make ceremony anew, to curate proper refuge. You contribute to the full metabolization of your life.

There is no time to lose. Begin now. Call a memory to your awareness. A moment from childhood when something miraculous to your small self happened. It could even be the delight of hearing the ice cream truck twinkle its way through your neighborhood. Recall what you felt most in touch with at the moment. The smells, the sounds, perhaps there was music coming from a radio. Maybe you had just been running through a sprinkler and were both hot from the summer sun and cool from the water pouring on your head. Ceremony is derived from the sensual.

To create ceremony from this moment only requires you to invoke those sensual elements, to overtly recognize the larger forces you are partnering with and the transmutation you desire to invoke.

In the ice cream truck scenario, you might realize that you want a ceremony that reanimates the energy of innocence and joy within you. You could recognize that your partners in this ceremony are the Sun and the Water Elemental. Every summer you could hold a ceremony where you gather friends together to pour water on your head in the heat of the day, play songs and eat ice cream while you each speak gratitude for the sun and share a memory of innocence. Ceremony need not be complicated. You need no one outside of you to create it. No outer forces are needed to consecrate the power that already lives within you. Ceremony is not to sanction or give permission. It is for celebration, affirmation and witness.

Receiving has a shadow form called greed. Without an ability to truly receive, hold and be changed by life, you only want more and more. Though you may technically "have" much, you reject it. You don't let it in and wake up feeling unfulfilled and empty. You become like the hungry ghosts from Tibetan Buddhist lore. These ghosts have huge mouths that constantly need to feed and huge bellies that are always empty. But they have tiny little throats, so very little ever passes through. You are constantly taking in information. But how much of it leaves a mark on your soul? What is all that consumption for?

The wisdom of the hungry ghost is that only by chewing food, breaking it down through tasting, meeting it with saliva and presence, can it pass through the tiny throat. Just as your food digests better when it is tasted and thoroughly chewed, your life metabolizes better when you turn your senses on. Feel what you are holding. Sense the way fabric lies on your skin. Hold the gaze of your lover.

A greater life is possible for you when you raise the standard in your life around receiving. You can begin right now to hold the standard that you only say yes to material that you can have genuine relationship with. This is not about limitation or minimalism. This is about revealing how much space - physically, psychically, emotionally, energetically, spiritually - can become available when you bring a new level of honesty to your ability to receive.

This is also why these identity shifts are so important—you are not meant to live at a static set point of your capacity for relationship. You are meant to wield the shakti of your desire to build the resilience required to relate to more.

Receiving is strange. To receive is to taste the flavor of the world anew. More than any mindset work, a life of receiving steeps you in the language of limitless abundance. Wealth becomes your undeniable reality.

Dreams reveal the mundane and mystical capacity to receive. Those dreams you've had where you've felt a degree of aliveness, a depth of love, an unshakable peace—unlike anything you've known in waking life—are preparing your persona for the power of greater receiving.

A common tool in manifestation is to visualize yourself as who you'd be once your vision is fulfilled. I invite you to do so now, but with the specific lens of: "When you are this person who has actualized the desire, how do you receive?"

You can comb the material of your dreams for clues. It can begin by remembering your first dream. Simply ask your consciousness to show you your first dream. No matter what dream surfaces, it is the correct one for this exercise.

The first dream I can recall was from the age of seven. In the dream I was with my sister in the bedroom we shared. I could fly. There was a feeling of freedom and elation in that dream that words cannot quite hold. And what I know is this: that when I am truly receiving, that is what it feels like.

Your persona will fight. It will continue to try to shutter the house of your being. The beauty of this is that there's nothing you need to do about it. The only task is to be with it. To receive the part of you that does not want to receive. You will then experience something wondrous.

This is the greatest magic of receiving—that when it becomes our default, we are blessed with gifts of which we are totally unaware.

By receiving the part of you that wants to reject life, you may also receive tremendous compassion and extreme gentleness. You may feel the tone of our yes and no come online.

The unwillingness to receive is simply an undernourished inner authority. The more presence you bring to this, the more you unlock the power of your choice. I can't say what you'll be blessed with. I can only tell you it's worth it to find out.

POEMS OF RECEIVING

1.

A Wholeness Pattern

I know what I am
I hide nothing
Hold nothing back
Resist nothing

This is how I am invisible
This is why you can't see me
How I become transparent
Hidden while held in view
I know what I am
I am enough
I am never enough
What is enough?
A heart with no metric
No need to confine and
define in this way.
Maps out of date
The moment they're drawn
It says, "Go right."
I go left only
For the joy that is in it
No wrong turns no matter
Where I go.

I know what I am
All pieces of me
I own

2.

This is why I am fearless
Nothing I seek to keep
From you

This is how I serve
Energy free from effort
to contort
I arrive fully for you
No part of me tethered
A Medusa of ancients
A wholeness pattern

I know what I am
That I can know what you are
That you can be seen in ways
You never have
A jailbreak for all that has been
Unloved
An ache in the bones
A dream that won't die
Truth shaking the ground
A voice shaky growing
Steady
A song we once knew here now
Re-memebered

I know what I am
That you can know
What you are

Love is
I am that
You are

3.

In honoring of the unseen

Thank you for this day of everything we don't know about. The unseen world that fills our lungs, our dreams, our spirits. The tints that color our view without our awareness.

Let us pause for a moment, breathe with all the babes in the womb, the soil microbes, the strands of virus and bacteria intelligence that are awakening and mobilizing something inside of us.

Thank you to everything we ignore, dismiss, downplay and avoid. The unforecast, unpredictable energies that give rise to surprise and newness.

4.

Sweet ancestors, move your breath in my circle.
Spiral your wisdom in me.
Bless the longing ache in my bones.
Rainbow you are—black, red, yellow, white, old, innocent, twice born, never born.
Your voice seeks my ear. Like a child I press close, listening for the inner sounds.
Instruct me in your harmony arts, invoke within me structures of peace. Lay my hands to the unfinished tasks. Find within me the missing pieces of the puzzle.
Open my heart generously to all my relations, practicing kindness wherever my foot falls. Help me to see your face in what I cannot understand. Show me the old ways of being a blessing to everyone I meet.
Walk me at your pace. Free me from hurry. Set me on a willing sprint for what nourishes this life.
Where I am a rookie elder, where I have walked the path further than some, imbue my teachings with the irreverent twinkling wisdom of you, like the stars that bless the sky.
Help me to find my place in the order of things, even as that order shifts and shuffles. Make my way one of honoring all that has gone before. Let me feel the feet that have cut the path.
There is no being human without being human together.
I am another you.
Ancient ones, help me to remember.

5.

The holy arc of life
Is held within your hands
Deep Power, you touch us in ways we can't see
You love us in unreasonable ways
You are the caress behind
The breeze on my face
You are the knowing in my bones
That aches so deep
It weeps its way through me
Erupts over my eyes and
spills through my lashes
You are the beauty I can't deny
The wonder that boldly combs through my days
The fleck of gold in my daughter's ancient feline eyes
The smattering freckles on my son's tanned and appled cheeks
The warm anchor of my lover's scent
The sudden acrobatics of Spider on my wall
You unfold conflict into intimacy
You show us what is shared
Beneath the wrongs we scold
I can't resist you
In my wild-haired youth
I scoured the ancient texts
I sought out ancient men
In ancient buildings
Searching for the Bodhisattva vow
Needles pressed it into my skin
A holy moment
A covenant

Held not only in words
But in flesh
Now
Every heartbeat
Belongs to you
My pulse tells the story
Of how
I'm yours
When you call, I answer
When I cry out
You are there
Unfailing, irresistible
There is no moment where you are not
Whatever concoctions of smallness I conjure
All the ways I look for suffering
Like a naive and innocent child
Fall apart in your fingers like sand
Float like ash
Beneath the lotus feet
Of your insane and unending and ecstatic dance
Your mercy brings light to what is
Dark in me
Not to heal it
But to bless it
Like a lover's touch
Tender leaves of new life
Spring from that place
Giving so fully
Receiving so fully
That the two become One

6.

What the wind taught me

Wind gathers
Pulls at my skirts
Rips branches from limbs
Causes moan-songs in structures
harmonizing their weight
A stillness inside me
It won't quit me
Noiseless, rock-solid, unmoving
Contrast
So much movement
Encircling such wild and stubborn quiet
I'm not like you
When you want to spin and run and go, go, go
Stones fall through my waters
Land soft and silent at the bottom
I'm not like you
I am you
Everything is its opposite
Like Neruda said
A breath so close that when you fall asleep
My eyes close
This nearness, raw intimacy
So alive that we try to take cover
We try to point at shapes and tones
As if contrast could
sever the bond.

Being Medicine

When you cry, my eyes fill
When you laugh my lips cheshire again
I'm not like you
You're not like me
We are not separate.
One animal, same breath
Inhale.
Exhale.
One life
seeking
To live

7.

Breathe it in.
Every deep breath an inhale of sunshine, the life force. Let it saturate and sing to every cell.
Breathe it in.
An inhale of wind, of the power of love, whispering a new day into your heart.
Let that Spirit that animates everything rise with the tide of your breath and draw out anything heavy, old, extra, not yours.
Let this breath inspire something different.
Listen to music that makes your body move.
Find something to wonder at.
Go into the open fields where no politics exist and life smiles at you.
Be silly even.
Let the love of this day find you, and carry you forward.

8.

My heart is so full with this day
With this sun
With soft sounds
With living waters
With naga dragons
With quietly powerful people
My heart is so full with this day
Beyond time
In the heart
Of aliveness
My heart is so full with this day
A day that brings you into
This world
Of light
Of deer talk
Of ravens wisdom
Of trees dancing
The beauty of this life
Is a celebration of you
And within you
It all lives
May the heart of this day
Be a smile
Reflecting back to you
The sacred wilderness
Of your presence here

9.

Today you said something kind
Today you gave energy to making someone else's life better
Today you made a tough decision
Today you breathed, even when you weren't noticing it!
Today people were feeling grateful for you; many, many more than you will ever know
Today the world is a better place because of you
The world is a better place today, not because you are perfect, but because you cared

10.

I've been off,
Crawling in the woods
And gazing at swan-flocked waves
Drumming and singing a new world into being.
Seven women.
Four days.
One cabin.
Heaven on earth.
I can't tell you how happy my heart is
at the thought of our next moment
As I returned home, a bald Eagle soared and swirled right above my car

11.

You are the gift
Your deepest love
Your yearning for
Something more than
You are living now
You are the gift
Notice what happens
When you show up to each
Person you love
Each person who
Irritates you
Each moment
Each breath
As the most precious gift
The gift that you are
When your heart's desire
Seems to be a far distant star
It helps to remember that space
Is the connective tissue
Of the universe
That which seems to separate us
Is actually what binds us together
When it's hard to walk the path before you
It helps to remember that though
The steps are unknown
Your destiny is certain

12.

When you are powerful
You deserve more love, not less
When you are exhausted
You deserve more love, not less
When you are misunderstood
You deserve more love, not less
When you are understood
You deserve more love not less
When everything is falling apart
You deserve more love, not less
When you have success
You deserve more love, not less
You are more powerful than your fear
You are more powerful than your excuses
You are more powerful than your job title
You are more powerful than your thoughts
And in all of this
You deserve more love,
Not less

13.

Space and time collapse in you
Nothing out of reach
Extending into endless
Layers

The portal to every world
Right here
Inside my own skin
What I once believe
Separated you and me
Is the depth of connection

Communion
It's all here
Now
Not you, not me, not us
Just aliveness
Here inside this skin

The dream door opens my heart.
I enter
Inner folds,
The heart of my heart.
Is you.

The moment I see, it is you.
I know you
Tell me the truth.
Always
I know, my heart.

You appear as
Whisper-born
From a far-distant star.

Cloud People announce
Your arrival.
Breezing
Whispering
Rolling tongues of smoke-language.

How long has it been?
How many lives have passed
Through this space
Between you and me?

Your name hasn't passed my lips for years.
Yet the moment I speak
Your words flash through.
Sheets of lightning sound
You will not lie to me.

I know you
Truth-teller, soothsayer, hierophant
Magi.
I forget
You
Re-member me.

14.

The way is open
What was far is nearer to me now
I approach it, I lean in, I listen
What will be, is now
I partner with dark sides of me
My secret strength
What I rejected
Now sits nearer to me
Hand in hand
Laughter
We move together
In the light
I am in the driver's seat
Pedal to the metal
The way is open
Hand in hand with delight
Expanding in space
The One Who Scowls
Is outside, far away
like a memory
On tip of tongue,
Far away, no bearing on this way.
The tiny softness of The Ally is with me
Sensing, smelling, touching, tasting, receiving
The way is open
The Ally rests
At my heart's back door
Her form
Innocent, breathing, dreaming

curled like a pup
There is a Mystery
It moves with me
From dream to dream
Nourishing
Seeds and sweetness
It is everywhere I go
It is what is
Made
From this open way

15.

In early infancy of morning
I walk across thawing earth
Smoke and salve tangling my hair
Each step
Breaking open
Portals in the
Uniform sheath
Ice crackling like laughter
The sun
Breaks open
Portals in my vision
As it walks across the sky
Portals of opening
Singing the old songs
That remember us
Into this:
Strength is not found by
What can I defend
Or
How expertly can I avoid
Strength is sourced
In what I birth
And set free

16.

Your voice is powerful.
Give it to praise today in whisper or laughter or roar.
Give with steadiness or with your knees shaking.
Let your voice and your choice shake the earth today with the joy that is your being.
Create the coming time of darker days as what your loving declares it to be, not what you fear says it could be.
Be bold, my friends. Be love.

17.

What happens in these moments?
These moments of more of less
That grow deeper and wider with each breath.
This breath, a shape that Spirit makes
When It touches the body.
A shape of softening
That widens us to touch
The realm of grief and hope
That open toward us now.
To spill fingers over its sharp and surprising
Edge.
Who do we become now?
With so much changed,
Some still moored, stuck, untouched.
A contracted form, voice tight.
Fighting the way we always fought.
Willing for or against, like always.
And yet, something bright and lit
And strange stirs within.
Now is the shape of something new.
New breath, breathing a new people.
New purpose, a purpose lived
Not held in concepts.
Sourced in our tissues
In our belonging
To blood and bone
To the clay earth and warm grass
To each other.
A purpose needing no understanding
Only to make its shape
Of love

18.

A flower is not
Trying to be somebody
It blooms without need for adoration
Praise
Confirmation

When we follow the fear path
We are led neurotically
Need to "be somebody"
To feel
Worthy

Come with me
Let's lose our minds
In the immensity and intensity
Of earth and sky
Let's bloom open
Because we can
Let's know the beauty
Of our unfolding
Taste the simple beauty
Of bringing
What you are
Who you have been
All along
See deeply into
Flower, bloom, tree, heart
Let it go
Let it go
Let it go

19.

Gazing out my window
Looking for her face
I find her
Attended by clouds that wind
Around her like snake
Draping her fullness
My ancestral song
Pulses through
My veins
Singing her name
She lives
She rises.

20.

When the grasses dry
I'll sit out on the earth
With you
In that field that Rumi says
Is out beyond right and wrong
We can sit until she remembers us.
We can sit until we hear the songs
Of our ancestors in our own breath
Just sitting and remembering the future
I'll drum for you like I used to
In the future
We'll laugh and roll on the ground
Like we used to
In the future
Our bodies will soften and we'll give our tears to the earth
Like we used to
In the future
We'll celebrate what it is to be alive
To put my hand in your heart
And put your hand in my heart
Like we used to
In the future

21.

Spider is renewal
Her mystery fangs it's way
Through blood and bone
What you seek
Does not run from you
It hunts you
Like the gods
Her hands are many
Her skill
Impeccable
Her silence
Undoing
Liquefying
Each stronghold
Of the past
I surrender to her whisper-ways now
I yield to her fortune
No season of my being
Untouched

22.

I taught my body how to feel love
(Or perhaps my body taught my mind its shape and sound)

Morning after morning, night into dream, my intention singular: to feel love for no reason, to partner with my gratitude as a way of being, a way of giving and receiving.

Now, when I wake, it's gratitude that meets me. The doors and windows of my heart already flung open. I don't have to manifest it. It manifests me.

My heart doesn't care what season it is in. A full bloom in February snow.

Now seas part before I raise my staff, the answer invites me to ask the question. The tightly woven threads of my reality fall apart as easily as Inanna drops her garments to go all the way down.

Now I dream, awake.

23.

A holding pattern
A pattern
Of holding, clinging, grasping
At some thing we called normal
Something as thick as air
As solid as space
This holding pattern
Was no living
At all
Now is a time to live
Into a beauty
So immediate that your body
Is pulled to it
Irresistible
This is no time to fight
No time to March
Or pledge allegiance to anything
That is less than
The souls song
That day
That day that she came back
She returned to us
In the shape of daughter
Fourteen
Soft and wise
That day
When we felt the terrible beauty
Of her
How she would rather die

Than not truly live
That day was a reckoning
That day she came home
From vision quest
Our loving laid bare
Everything non-essential stripped away
The light of her life
Her aliveness
The spark of her wild
Is with us once more

RITUAL FOR RECEIVING

Follow the QR code to receive a deeper instruction on creating your personal ceremony of receiving. Play with the questions below to deepen.

JOURNAL PROMPTS FOR RECEIVING

What can I allow to touch me now?

How can I let it in deeper?

What do I want to consecrate, honor and affirm within my life?

What has gone unwitnessed in me?

How do I receive in my most intimate moments, such as in sex?

What are the institutions I no longer affirm?

What wants to be more thoroughly tasted by me?

Where am I holding, but not receiving?

What could change if I gave it to myself?

Epilogue

This book is the dream I dreamed for you. Dreams are a communication, a symbolic language of soul. They provide a perspective on daily consciousness that individuals and communities, have forgotten or have dissociated from.

Dreams are not literal but ask us to dwell deep in the layers of our heart, to put our hands there and feel for what is really true now.

For most of human history, dreaming was understood as a sacred ground of insight, wisdom and healing. Our ancient relatives did not think dreaming to be a random assortment of nighttime happenings that were simply the brain organizing and cleaning itself. They knew the realms of dreams are every bit as real as our own. They knew them as a place of medicine, healing and insight.

I am a dreamer. I dream for healing. I dream for guidance. I dream for my clients and my loved ones.

I dream for you.

In the long-ago times, when a woman or man didn't know what to do, a sister would say, "Let me dream on that for you."

Show me what I need to know.

Show me what we need to know.

I dreamed this for you. I invite you to read it again and again, as if it was precisely just for you alone. Because it is. Notice what you feel in your body. Notice what has you leaning in or pulling away.

I don't dream for the sake of dreaming. I dream so my choices and actions remain rooted in truths and yearnings that might otherwise become drowned and lost to me if I only ever look outside for what is real.

I dream because it is the most reliable tool I have to access courage, create coherence, to bring lost soul parts home and be impeccable in my service.

I dream as medicine because the actions it guides me to take scare the shit out of me; not because I act them out literally, but because dreams let us feel all the things we are unwilling to feel and open up aspects of deeper living the daylight blinds us to.

I dreamed this for you, that we may be free.

Let it be so for you.

Let it be so for me.

Let it be so for us all.

RITUAL FOR CLOSURE

All true containers have a beginning and an end. To signify the end of this particular walk around the Wheel, I invite you into a simple ritual.

In ancient times and in some places still today, when a young woman began her monthly bleeds a ceremony would be held to sanctify and bless her womanhood. The puberty rites of boys in traditional society often involve the men of the tribe "stealing" the boy from his mother and ritually beating him. This is not a sick power move. It is to instill the wisdom into the boy that, as a man, he will face things larger than himself. He will experience pain.

A young woman already knows pain as she comes into womanhood. Her monthly bleed provides it. The women of the tribe would gather around the initiate and cut a circle around her navel, leaving a scar. This was to remind the initiate that she is the Whole. She is total. All of life flows from her. She finds her place in the community of life by remembering it comes from her.

To bring the Wheel to a close, to acknowledge that all the archetypes of woman are alive, valid and potent within you, find a nontoxic marker and draw a circle around your navel. Life comes from you. Manifesting your life from within is your deepest gift to us all.

About the Author

Juliet Trnka is a coyote shaman, mother, lover, CEO of Direct Knowing, poet and author of *Being Medicine*. Her work centers on supporting women in living fully, unapologetically and abundantly through intimate partnership with multidimensional, sacred tools. She writes to honor the coyote dreams within you that have gone unheard and unfollowed until now.

Made in the USA
Monee, IL
12 November 2023